Inventing
Socrates

BY THE SAME AUTHOR

The Pilgrim City
Saint Augustine of Hippo: An Intellectual Biography

Inventing Socrates

Miles Hollingworth

Bloomsbury Academic
An imprint of Bloomsbury Publishing Inc

B L O O M S B U R Y
NEW YORK · LONDON · NEW DELHI · SYDNEY

Bloomsbury Academic
An imprint of Bloomsbury Publishing Inc

1385 Broadway	50 Bedford Square
New York	London
NY 10018	WC1B 3DP
USA	UK

www.bloomsbury.com

BLOOMSBURY and the Diana logo are trademarks of Bloomsbury Publishing Plc

First published 2015

© Miles Hollingworth, 2015

All rights reserved. No part of this publication may be reproduced or transmitted in any form or by any means, electronic or mechanical, including photocopying, recording, or any information storage or retrieval system, without prior permission in writing from the publishers.

No responsibility for loss caused to any individual or organization acting on or refraining from action as a result of the material in this publication can be accepted by Bloomsbury or the author.

ISBN: HB: 978-1-6235-6303-5
PB: 978-1-6235-6448-3
ePub: 978-1-6289-2664-4
ePDF: 978-1-6289-2665-1

Library of Congress Cataloging-in-Publication Data
Hollingworth, Miles.
Inventing Socrates / Miles Hollingworth.
pages cm
Includes bibliographical references and index.
ISBN 978-1-62356-303-5 (hardback : alk. paper) –
ISBN 978-1-62356-448-3 (pbk. : alk. paper) – ISBN 978-1-62892-664-4 (ePub) –
ISBN 978-1-62892-665-1 (ePDF) 1. Pre-Socratic philosophers. 2. Philosophy, Ancient–Influence. 3. Philosophy and religion. 4. Philosophy and science. I. Title.
B187.5.H65 2015
182–dc23
2015005747

Typeset by Integra Software Services Pvt. Ltd.

To Dad
– For all the conversations that stayed the course

CONTENTS

1 Predestination 1
2 The Way of Truth 37
3 The Soul of Blood 71
4 The Fatal Masks 125

Notes 149

Bibliography 162

Index 166

1

Predestination

*O my body! I dare not desert the likes of you in other men
and women, nor the likes of the parts of you,
I believe the likes of you are to stand or fall with the likes
of the soul, (and that they are the soul,)*
WALT WHITMAN

What is the American poet Walt Whitman doing here at the head of Chapter 1 of a book, ostensibly on Presocratic philosophy? Why, for that matter, is this chapter titled 'Predestination'? The whole rest of this book must be the full explanation, but I can get at the essence of it now in a kind of opening manifesto.

Now, more than ever they have been, the classic foundations of the Western tradition are in a position to send us some of the up-to-the-minute news of today's world. Not too long ago, Western ideas and their relationship to social and political life were still in the thrills and momentums of the big experiments around the world. I mean experiments like the new world of America; the empires of Europe; and the declarations of human rights. The confidence behind all of these was their belief in the good life as a kind of religion. This Western style of worshipping whatever can stand to reason in the world seemed like a perfect and unimpeachable practice – borne out by a happy conjunction between the actual tactility of the laws of nature and the wilful selflessness of Christian values. 'Altruism' was what it saw each morning when it put on its uniform and looked in the mirror. Rationality was the true egalitarianism, and science and judgements of fact (the same everywhere) the ultimate proof of this. But mighty and reasonable as all of it has been, there is something that this tradition has always known and experienced and esteemed, but which it has had no natural way of accounting for in theory. This is the soul. The human soul has been there at work in every human culture there ever has been. Yet now it looks increasingly like it was better and more instinctively handled in the more ancient cultures of the world. Or indeed, in their counterparts in the present world – the cultures of the undeveloped world, with their undiminished sense for what can be called pantheism or anthropomorphism, but which is really a healthy regard for the fundamental needs of human sight lines.

No human being can at heart want to be a calculating machine. It is true that what Whitman calls the likes and the parts of us in other men and women can, on one view, be worked up into a classification scheme and a theory of knowledge. But that is not what he meant by his joyful lament: and we, too, seem to be living today in a popular culture in the West that is hankering once again after ritual, symbolism, code and conspiracy. At any rate, for some reassurance that after all this hard intelligence and number crunching, there may be some experience left to be had of the seeing that doesn't go through things in the way that reductionism goes through things, but which activates our sensuality – and sensuality's possessiveness.

The Western eye has been conditioned into the dogma that its interface with the world is to be Dewey Decimal and archival. Items are picked up and seen at precisely the same time as they are catalogued and put into their proper place. What we can all look forward to one day, so this posturing goes, will be various versions of augmented reality. But this is a conflicted dogma, at odds with the authentic and original truth-experience that, say, Whitman was after. This is the idea that the most valuable and unencumbered form of knowing that there is, is the way that you can feel your corporeal self animated and stabbed-through by frightening, tightening pangs of possessiveness. 'The philosopher and every wise man, loves truth, loves reason' – here is meant to be the sane and proper beginning for every pukka house of ideas. But before the soul ever loved reason, she was a lover plain and wild. And that was her spirit. And this means that before repression, or sublimation, or the good life, or whatever you want to call it, there is this that must always come first in any worthy assessment of who we are. And 'this that must always come first' must also therefore sit in a region that can be described by neither right nor wrong: for its striking feature is that it is playing like hair triggers on the kinds of things you would die for. Her head on your shoulder. The way she picked you out from all the world. Your children. Your brother. Your homeland. Its breeze on your face. All of these things exist in the world that came first, before theory came along. A world unashamed by all these things it lusted for, and indeed its self-love in lusting for them. Theory is how we blush, and try to fix this, and make all things work together for good, whatever 'good' is. But now I have a strong suspicion that for one reason or another, we have come full circle and reawakened our desire to return to this world that came first.

It encourages me to say quite openly that the Presocratics, and how they invented Socrates, are going to be our story once again – its best and its worst bits. We don't have to read them any longer from any kind of respectful distance; indeed we shouldn't given what I have been saying. For if the history of philosophy has been like a cabinet full of trophies, meant to make us feel better about ourselves and proud, then that is also *all* that it has been – alone and inanimate in a corner. Which is a shame because I believe that the story of how Socrates was invented was a psychological episode; and that for this reason it can be gone through again (by us and continuously) with materials of the natural and supernatural that we discover within ourselves. Within ourselves this morning, if we like.

A strange romance

Even though it is still early days, let me summarize what I have been saying, so that there can be no misunderstanding. The European adventure of ideas seems to me to be a strange romance. It is the romance of an honourable intention. It is on behalf of all men and women. It is not the romance of the home and the hearth, which is yours and yours alone by the sheer fact that it is no one else's. The romance of the home and the hearth is apolitical in its originality and partiality – it is unrecognizable to anyone save its owner. It is your wife, but not *qua* Woman; it is your husband, but not *qua* Man. So when it has to be recognized as anything wider than this, it tends to be recognized politically, in terms of your legal rights and freedoms to ownership and enjoyment of it as a category concept – and then again in terms of those rights' protection by the State. But to notice this is not to speak against this strange romance. There is no question that there is something genuinely noble and uplifting about, yes, political freedom in the West. But between this and the romance you can feel for what is yours and yours alone, there is a chasm of difference that can never be crossed.

There is, of course, an immediate answer to give at this point, which is a true answer. This is the answer of moral pluralism. In a properly constituted society of today, private citizens are no longer agents but spaces – spaces which are theirs to fill with their opinions and preferences. It is not the business of the State to impinge on the home and the hearth. Moral pluralism creates an atmosphere in which the romance of the home and the hearth can flourish. It is its guarantor and protector, and achieves this on its terms of operation. No, what I am pushing for with all my Whitman-talk about pre-rational sight lines and loves is something that belongs to the deep-private and the deep-subjective, but which can only be pointed to in relief like this against the apparatus of the State. On the one hand, you have to accept and admire that it is written into the very definition of the modern state that it should seek as little as possible to judge such inner things as I am intimating. But on the other hand, there is the problem that whilst statehood and civilization may have set up the pools and channels in which the blood of life has been able to settle and flow, this same settling and flowing has never brought us a step closer to understanding what lifeblood actually *is*. Neither has the painstaking measuring and describing of the pools and channels. Clearly, I suspect that Whitman knew what lifeblood is, and I am grateful to have his lyrical example for my book. For my part, I strongly suspect that by cracking open and reliving an episode like the birth of philosophy, we will get a little closer to realizing why it is now – in the year 2015 – that we are thirsting for lifeblood ourselves once again.

The Western tradition is therefore in the unusual situation of having its achievements as well as its shames derive from the same source. In the firstborn sense, it 'owns' the unmistakable idea that there is such a thing as free, reasoned thought – followed as its own imperative. This idea says that if you are a human being, wherever you are, and whatever situation you happen to be in, you owe it to yourself to cast off all your other imperatives to action and educate yourself into this one. What could be wiser than that? But at the same time, this evangelical zeal has furnished the world with the never-to-be-forgotten image of the colonial administrator and the notion of the 'white man's burden'. For a time this was very nearly indistinguishable from Western Christianity in mission throughout the world. But now, when its traditional religion is no longer being allowed this same status as the safeguard and vanguard of values and institutions, what the West prefers to be seen to be exporting are the plain civil liberties of good governance and behaviour. Nevertheless, for those wanting it, the sense of shame can linger on in the question whether the Western way of life can be justified in its promotion to other cultures as something superior to what they already have, developed to undeveloped; or in their own best interests, if they could only see them.

I do, though, want to have gone on record at this point as having said the following. In most cases where the Western way rides in to save the day, one is facing a moot, if not an absolutely irrelevant, question. There are situations in the world so desperate, so war-ravaged or simply so poverty-stricken that help for its own sake is all that is required – and Western nations happen to be in the position to give that help. So fair enough that it should be on their terms.

Something else too. The traditional, ethical language of freedom has made it out to be the virtue as wide as the very institution of democracy itself – or for that matter, of justice itself or society itself. But when you think about it, what we instinctively feel freedom to be has never been any such giant, catch-all prizes as these, but instead a succession of moments. Freedom, like marriage, is a sacrament that only ever seems to belong to the two bodies that go into making each of its moments. In the case of freedom, these are the oppressor and the oppressed. To anyone else looking on and speculating from the outside in, however clever or well informed they might be, freedom, like marriage, is just going to have to be a stranger to them. I mean that they will have to wait their turn, and retell its story through their own bodies. And this, we might agree, is appropriate: for things as important as freedom can only take off into their true feeling and meaning when they become possible to be recounted as your personal testimony. No amount of theory can ever prepare you for what it's really going to be like because (again) not one jot of theory ever came first. Theory has always been in this position of coming after the fact of whatever it is pontificating about. It is the voyeur attitude. When, in his memoirs, Henry Kissinger tried to defend the general activities of American foreign policy on his watch, he dropped everything, went instinctive in this way I mean and went back to what freedom had first meant to him:

> When I was a boy [America] was a dream, an incredible place where tolerance was natural and personal freedom unchallenged. Even when I learned later that America, too, had massive problems, I could never forget what an inspiration it had been to the victims of persecution, to my family, and to me during cruel and degrading years. I always remembered the thrill when I first walked the streets of New York City. Seeing a group of boys, I began to cross to the other side to avoid being beaten up. And then I remembered where I was.[1]

The Presocratics are so-called because they were the first philosophers in the West up to Socrates. The significance of Socrates as a watershed is that whilst the Presocratics are primarily said to have been interested in the phenomena of the physical world, Socrates represents the humanistic turn in philosophy. With him, philosophy became taken up with the business of human flourishing – or the 'good life', what is also called the science of living well. If the Presocratics were walking around today, we should probably call them scientists rather than philosophers on account of the distinction that we now make between these two disciplines. Science is something we generally think of as indistinguishable from its methods. These methods allow us to have clear ideas about the form and ethos of the answer that science will give to a problem, even if we haven't yet worked out precisely what the content of that answer is going to be. Philosophy is rather a different kettle of fish. It is the tool we take up for those big, more or less irresolvable problems of life. The classics: like 'What is the key to happiness?' or 'What does the just society look like?' In fact, when you look at the perennially contested nature of these questions, you also realize that philosophy is less about arriving at pinpoint, empirical solutions than about helping us to reach intellectually respectable opinions. The popular image of Socrates as the bearded sage is testament to this difference.

By and large, the Presocratics felt that they were in the business of seeking out the underlying reasons for the way that our Cosmos is as it is. So we call them philosophers because this means that they were seeking rational explanations behind the giant goings-on that the natural world was facing them with. And we think of them as pioneering this acceleration of thought because behind them lay the older, more magical forms of explanation that they were rejecting in order to pursue their way. But insofar as their relationship to Socrates goes, it has long been traditional to do what I have just done – and insert this caveat about them being more like modern-day scientists on account of their primary interest in the empirical, inanimate world. Aristotle, who seems to have cultivated a good knowledge of his forerunners, had the following to say about this distinction in his *Metaphysics*:

> Most of those who first philosophized thought that in the materials of things would be found their only beginnings or principles. That from which all beings come, that from which they first arise and into which they last go, the primary being persisting through its many transformations, this it is, they say, that is elemental and primary in things. Hence they think that nothing is either originated or destroyed, since such a nature is always conserved; just as we say that Socrates neither is originated absolutely when he becomes beautiful or educated, nor is he destroyed when he loses those traits, because the Socrates in whom these changes occur remains. So, too, nothing else is originated or destroyed without qualification; for there must be a nature, whether one or more than one, out of which things are generated, but which itself endures.[2]

Then again, there are the obvious reasons why the Presocratics wouldn't really be able to pass as scientists today. The first of them, Thales, was born in Miletus in the seventh century B.C. – in the region of ancient Greece called Ionia, or what is today Izmir Province in Turkey. The last of them, Diogenes, was from Apollonia in Thrace – or present-day Sozôpol in Bulgaria. He was known to have been flourishing around the first part of the fifth century B.C. In between and including these two men are usually counted altogether seventeen philosophers. Of course, things are never as tight and neat as this. At one end, it remains an open question for scholarship quite how one can say that modern philosophical thinking began, of a sudden, with Thales. Clearly something did begin with him; but common sense warns us that the birth of an intellectual phenomenon like Western philosophy must have been preceded by a long period of gestation in the womb. Here, this 'womb' consists of ancient religion and myth; and true enough, the ideas and theories of the Presocratics have all by now been shown by scholarship to build upon and develop the emotional confidence of Greek literature and art. And at the other end to this, we find that Diogenes' flourishing around 440–430 B.C. would have actually made him a contemporary of Socrates. So here, too, the termini break down. Additionally, there is the fact that it is now possible to include along the way a handful of women philosophers, ordinarily left off the lists. The most well known notwithstanding being Theano (believed to have been Pythagoras' wife) and her daughters, Myia, Damo and Arignote.[3] Their feminine take on affairs becomes especially important given the innate sexuality of Presocratic thought. That is to say, the Presocratics belonged to a long lost age in which sex was not the battleground it is today. For them, it was the major theme and power in the symphony of men, gods and nature that they were watching play out before them. They were its glad and fortunate subjects and could never have imagined the attitude of our popular conception of it, in which we overmaster and control it, the better to make it just another of the sweets in the jar. The point of sex, to them, was rather that it was the boldest of the hands that Fate plays with. Just two cards, male and female: but so many shades of each: and who should go to whom? To get into the Presocratic mind on this, think of true love. People are finding it with each other all the time, yet given all the billions of people on this earth, what are the chances of that? Fate must be a mighty and terrible goddess to manage this matchmaking. Or I am speaking of ghosts, and nonsense, and there is no such thing as true love but only biology and itch and impulse. Let me at any rate quote Parmenides for the Presocratic side here:

The narrower rings were filled with unmixed fire, those next to them with night, and after them rushes their share of flame; and in the midst of them is the Goddess who steers all; for she it is that begins all the works of hateful birth and begetting, sending female to mix with male and male in turn with female.[4]

And:

On the right boys, on the left girls ... [5]

In these matters and others, the Presocratics show, time and again, that they are the masters of symbolism – of how a few deftly sketched connections can join the dots within our parts. We are in the habit of saying that 'wonder', that most human of abilities, is motivated by a desire to understand and grasp things not yet owned – things outside and independent of us. But the truth is that we are only able to wonder because of that which has already been written inside of us. At its symbolist best, this amounts to the knowledge that the mystery of all mysteries is the spark of life: for with this spark the impossible becomes possible, and the full magic of consciousness, soul and individuality become born from the utterly generic materials of seed and egg. Shortly after it comes the next mystery of mysteries: this is the despatch of life into its male and female forms. Last of all is how we are capable of bringing reflection back upon this: and knowing instinctively that there is poetry to be written between the impetuosity and expendability of man and the forbearance and guardianship of woman – I mean her guardianship over Wisdom, whose soil, it seems, is the only soil into which a man can plant the flag of his ambition. By and large the delicacy of this has been lost in the thrusting philosophies of post-industrial societies. Native American philosophy preserves a beautiful and chastening reminder of it. In the Hopi rendering of the creation myth, the gods create a kind of demiurge called 'Spider Woman' or 'Thinking Woman' on account of her god-given ability to walk on and tend to the complex interconnectedness of all things, human and natural. She does not conquer but teaches; and may even sit still in the ear of a warrior, so that, if he is properly attentive, it is *her* words of wisdom that may save him from his pounding blood.[6]

Occasionally, though, post-industrial societies do throw up stark new ways for this delicacy of difference to be experienced. Ernest Hemingway, in his short story *A Natural History of the Dead*, once wrote of the impression made on him by a terrible industrial accident at an Italian munitions factory. He called his impression 'the inversion of the usual sex of the dead':

> Regarding the sex of the dead it is a fact that one becomes so accustomed to the sight of all the dead being men that the sight of a dead woman is quite shocking. I first saw inversion of the usual sex of the dead after the explosion of a munitions factory which had been situated in the countryside near Milan, Italy ... I must admit, frankly, the shock it was to find that these dead were women rather than men.[7]

As recently as 1994, a new fragment of the Presocratic philosopher Empedocles was discovered, in which he writes about Love and Strife as formative principles of the universe; and in which he invokes these deep quivering rhythms that I am talking about. He also throws his message open to be received by all the human senses at once, 'not only your ears', but the eyes – the judges of beauty, the gateways to longing.

> But when Strife reaches transgressively the depths of the vortex, and Love comes to be at the middle of the whirlpool, then under her [i.e. Love] do all these things [i.e. elements] come together to be only one. Exert yourself – so that the account reach not only your ears – and as you listen look upon the unerring evidences that are around you. I will show your eyes, too, where things [i.e. elements] find a larger body: first the coming together and unfolding [i.e. proliferation] that breeding consists in, and all the variety that is now still left in this phase of generation, whether among the wild species of mountain roaming beasts, or with the twin offspring of humans [i.e. the two sexes], or with the progeny of root-bearing fields and the cluster of grapes mounting upon the vine. From these accounts convey to your mind undeceitful proofs: for you will see the coming together and unfolding that breeding consists in.[8]

For all these reasons, it becomes clear that the Presocratics belong to a period of Western history kept firmly apart from our own. To go back to their time B.C. is to journey into what we have been educated to imagine is the naive pre-history to our own great success. With the Presocratics begins something that we are now in the fortunate position of being able to give its finishing touch – to polish and to stand back from to admire. Because for all that they were doing to produce cosmologies that could stand to reason, the Presocratics could display a dismaying allegiance to the ancient belief that the world of humans is also populated with gods and spirits. They took these beliefs for granted and ran them side by side, and confusingly, with the very critical thinking that we want to applaud them for. I have mentioned Thales as the first of these first philosophers, and he can now provide a standout example of this. Thales believed that water was in some way the elemental key to all things, and in this we can detect a genuine proto-science, however murky.

> For moist natural substance, since it is easily formed into each different thing, is accustomed to undergo very various changes: that part of it which is exhaled is made into air, and the finest part is kindled from air into aither, while when water is compacted and changes into slime it becomes earth. Therefore Thales declared water, of the four elements, was the most active, as it were, as a cause.[9]

But at the same time, his explanation of the phenomenon of magnetism appeared to be this:

> Thales, too, seems, from what they relate, to have supposed that the soul was something kinetic, if he said that the (Magnesian) stone possesses soul because it moves iron.[10]

And worse:

> Thales said that the mind of the world is god, and that the sum of things is besouled, and full of daimons; right through the elemental moisture there penetrates a divine power that moves it.[11]

This sort of thing is most dismaying, or indeed most confirming, to those intellectuals today who maintain that religion is something that we are duty-bound to step out of when once we have seen it for what it is. Duty-bound in the sense that to remain in so ancient and retarding a habit of mind would be to commit real and wilful violence against the progress of mankind – even if only for utilitarian reasons of sentimentality, rootedness and comfort. One of the most outspoken of these recently has been A. C. Grayling. In his book *The God Argument: The Case* against *Religion and* for *Humanism*, he puts it like this:

> [T]he case against religion goes deeper than an argument for secularism. It is that religion's claims and beliefs do not stand up to examination. Briefly put, critical examination of religion's claims places it in the same class as astrology and magic. Like these systems of thought, religion dates from mankind's less educated and knowledgeable early history, and like them it has been superseded by advances in our understanding of the world and ourselves.[12]

This question of what can and should stand up to examination in the respectable life of today is a broad reminder that what buttresses the bullishness of this outlook is the belief that human history is always the history of development. When we 'tell' a history involving humans – any history involving humans – we expect to be able to tell it in terms of milestones. To take the example of this book, I have already made it clear that the Presocratics have long been regarded by scholars as the 'first philosophers', so that their story has traditionally been told as the story of the 'birth of Western philosophy'. But it has to be considered at the same time that to do this may simply serve to indicate some trait of 'Western thought', whatever 'Western' can mean. It may be that other peoples do not make this same assumption that linear time is to be measured in increments of intellectual, cultural and technological advancement. I think, in particular, of how it has remained an unresolved issue for the Western mind that it has no *natural* way of approaching other peoples deemed to be at more primitive stages than it. Isn't the classic dilemma for the anthropologist still the dilemma of 'first contact' – to document, but not to change?

Over the jungle

White people appear over the jungles in helicopters and the brown people run away: and the white people conclude that the brown people will stop running away if only they can be educated into what a helicopter really is (not a giant bird or a whirling dervish). Like a flash, these thoughts, repeated over and over in the course of Western history, have allowed the White Mind to regard itself as the first born of reason, and to regard its education as irreproachable and the same thing as truth.

Now I want to ask, What is going to happen if I choose here to return the counter-truth and say that it is only because we have helicopters that we can have our knowledge of what a helicopter really is? Because I suspect that when you look at it like this, and isolate and challenge the notion of linear advancement at the heart of the matter, you are going to see that the possession of knowledge is accidental – yes, accidental right down to the very accident of birth that has put some of us in the helicopter and some of us in the jungle. Yet white book wisdom continues to regard itself as the worldwide paradigm of truth. And it encourages us to speak as though tribes remain undiscovered until they are discovered. And then having been discovered, it encourages us to subject them to the notebook and the pen, and explain them back to themselves; as though they had all along been unaware that what they were doing was really an example of 'behaviour X', where behaviour X has been observed in other animals in similar situations. The head hunter and the peacock both wanted something to display.

But please don't think that my point is that facts accumulated in this way are useless and unimportant. There is no question that we are materially better off in a first world standard of life. And there is even less question that those who strive to bring it to us, and beyond us, to bring it to those who don't yet have it, are performing a sincere work of mercy. What better argument could you muster for this than the benefits of Western medicine? But only by using such uncompromising language as I am can I draw attention to the possibility – and I don't mean it to be any more than 'the possibility' for the purposes of this book – that what is regarded as the calm dispassion and purity of Western intellection (its universal gift to the world) is what rather too quickly evolves into its mandate to be propagated and preached. And at this point enters the tricky business of human nature. For if the Western mind has indeed had the luck to be the first born of reason (to be the first to fly around in helicopters), how should it then handle this knowledge and continue to remind itself that what it has benefitted from has been no more than a slice of luck? Which is the same thing as to say that, if its science is unquestionably *true*, so that any human being anywhere would be able to grasp it and affirm its truth with the requisite enlightenment, how can it retain any moral possession of it – when 'it' is on this definition the universal possession of humankind? Because of course 'possession' and 'human nature' do matter here. They matter very much. For while truth and education may contain these features that indicate that they should be everybody's by right, there is that other right which intervenes – the right to property and to the lawful earnings of one's sweat. The problem for the West is that it has no way of separating its luck as the first born of reason from the hard work and values of its societies (the (American) dream). And you are entitled to say that it shouldn't have to. In fact to call what I am describing a 'problem' is probably too strong a word.

If the first-world-way was waiting all along to be discovered by men and women who would do no more, in effect, than notice and exploit the laws of nature that entail it, then its secret is nobody's secret and its truth is nobody's property. As indeed the proofs and theorems of mathematics are nobody's property, which leaves us with the uniquely human dilemma that we all know so well. The West has worked hard to enjoy and be proud of a success that it can measure in material and territorial terms. It has regarded it as sin to leave a stone unturned or a field untilled. It has grown up, through this, into a paternalistic, magnanimous outlook on the world. Yet there have always been those to point the finger and say that there is something a little too convenient about this chiasm of science – empire – and the (gift of the) rights of man (to the world).

On the one hand, the Western mind must respect the sovereignty of those it meets in the field and be the intrigued and disquieted observer. The following example from Elspeth Huxley's book about her time among the Kikuyu of Kenya shows exactly what I mean:

> I felt like a missionary tormented by the sight of thousands of innocent souls perishing merely because they lacked the words that would have saved them. When I pointed to the sky in which

the red had all but faded and said: 'Look, it is good,' which was the only word available, they glanced up politely, nodded, and one said: 'Yes, it is good,' and went on with his conversation. Perhaps he had words for his feelings, and his feelings were like mine, but I could never know, and this, too, was disquieting.[13]

On the other hand, to stand back and resist the temptation to 'save' and 'educate' can be deemed to be unacceptable from another point of view. Here the project of Western history has been made to squirm on the charge that it has systematically neglected the higher calling of its peculiar adventure of ideas. The question at the bottom of this charge has always been the same. Is a free-market distribution of ideas, religions and goods a sacrosanct ideal in itself, and therefore a genuine discovery, or is it really a neutral description of a state of affairs that arose, over time and in certain circumstances, in Europe and afterwards in America? In other words, What can accurately be defended in it – a true and perfect realization of freedom or the right to a way of life, historically prone to empire-building and absolved (on the logic of its mechanism) from too great responsibility for its end results? In this sense, the Western mind is continuously being called to examine its conscience in ways that other cultures avoid. I am suggesting that this is the price that it has to pay for proclaiming to operate in the name of 'objective truth'. It cannot simply live and let live. Everyone is waiting to jump on the hypocrisies that spring up in the gap between what it does and the ethical language it uses afterwards to vindicate what it has done. One of the best and most succinct summaries of this critical mood that faces the West comes from the Algerian revolutionary and writer Frantz Fanon – and his book *The Wretched of the Earth*:

> All the elements of a solution to the great problems of humanity have, at different times, existed in European thought. But Europeans have not carried out in practice the mission which fell to them, which consisted of bringing their whole weight to bear violently upon these elements, of modifying their arrangement and their nature, of changing them and, finally, of bringing the problem of mankind to an infinitely higher plane.[14]

It gets even worse for the West when you factor in its long involvement with Christianity and Christian principles of good living. At various times, Western statesmen have been moved to suggest that the principal features of their politics replicate certain of the Christian imperatives to just behaviour and honest striving; yet everybody knows that the Christian anthropology of fallen man contains within itself the seeds of a damning critique of Mammon – a critique that is founded upon the recognition that the human person has spiritual *as well as* material needs, and that the former cannot be properly satisfied by a diet of utopian principles derived from the latter. Famous in this regard was the British historian R. H. Tawney and his pioneering study *Religion and the Rise of Capitalism*. Here is his withering conclusion:

> The shaft of Mephistoles, which drops harmless from the armour of Reason, pierces the lazy caricature which masquerades beneath that sacred name, to flatter its followers with the smiling illusion of progress won from the mastery of the material environment by a race too selfish and superficial to determine the purpose to which its triumphs shall be applied. Mankind may wring her secrets from nature, and use their knowledge to destroy themselves; they may command the Ariels of heat and motion, and bind their wings in helpless frustration, while they wrangle over the question of the master whom the imprisoned genii shall serve. Whether the chemist shall provide them with the means of life or with tri-nitro-toluol and poison gas, whether industry shall straighten the bent back or crush it beneath heavier burdens, depends on an act of choice between incompatible ideals, for which no increase in the apparatus of civilization at man's disposal is in itself a substitute.[15]

There is no point in me going on beyond Tawney's conclusion, because I think the thought I wanted to nurture between him, Huxley and Fanon is now quite as clear as it needs to be. In her 1968 work *Between Past and Future*, Hannah Arendt suggested that the classical languages of ethics and virtue can no longer diagnose the modern situation – that, intellectually speaking, we now live in more or less post-moral societies, in which it has become unfashionable anymore to think of civilization as like a DNA that Socrates and Plato and Aristotle uncovered for us once upon a time. There is now too much of a stigma – the opposite of self-determination – in acquiescing like children in the tradition which they laid down for us. Neither, for that matter, did Arendt think that we should want to round on this situation in the Marxist way; for if the idea of civilization as like a DNA brings us unacceptably close to intellectual conservatism, and wisdom literatures of infinite future applicability, and all the supernatural trajectory of this, then Marxism goes too far in the opposite direction. In the effort to break us from this aristocratic past and find a new moral dimension in the economic stages of life, it does even greater damage to human responsibility. It becomes eschatology without even a god, which is the same thing, in practice, as politics without even a country.

When Arendt was writing, everything seemed to hang on establishing what could flourish in between this 'past' and 'future'. It seemed like a unique opportunity to relearn the sense in which, to the Western Psyche, freedom must always be experienced as the activity of 'freethinking'. Freethinking by thinkers like the Presocratics had allowed the classical tradition to emerge from what had gone before it of spirits and dream songs. More freethinking by Christian intellectuals like Paul and Augustine had provided the next inrush of insight – what Arendt called the 'murderous dialectics of the heart'. Namely: the experience of freedom described in terms of a continuous cannoning between what we would (in a higher mind) do and the thing that prevents us from doing what we would which is (by Christianity) called 'sin'. Finally, she had noticed how the reductionist accounts of the human condition like Marx's (however beguilingly simple they could seem in relation to all this introspection and doom) were in fact a treacherous betrayal because in effect they plotted to impose over our free wills the inevitabilities of material and scientific processes, inevitabilities to which we should in any case have to submit to let these theories run true – *post hoc ergo propter hoc*. The problem – as Arendt saw it then – was that no mere human contrivance for happiness, or the good life, can ever truly be what we mean by 'freethinking', or 'free will'. By the same token, this freedom can therefore never be imagined to be something that could have been learned within the historical conditions of human association. It is much rather like the rocket engine that allows us to periodically remember ourselves: and remembering ourselves, and what it should mean to be human, to escape the very gravity of things like tradition, and Christianity, and Marxism. It is much rather like an existential declaration of *being*: and should therefore be sought in that sense, however tricky such a freedom might then be to reconcile with peaceful human society. In Arendt's words,

> [T]he greatest difficulty in reaching an understanding of what freedom is arises from the fact that a simple return to tradition, and especially to what we are wont to call the great tradition, does not help us. Neither the philosophical concept of freedom as it first arose in late antiquity, where freedom became a phenomenon of thought by which man could, as it were, reason himself out of the world, nor the Christian and modern notion of free will has any ground in political experience. Our philosophical tradition is almost unanimous in holding that freedom begins where men have left the realm of political life inhabited by the many, and that it is not experienced in association with others but in intercourse with one's self – whether in the form of an inner dialogue which, since Socrates, we call thinking, or in a conflict within myself, the inner strife between what I would and what I do, whose murderous dialectics disclosed first to Paul and then to Augustine the equivocalities and impotence of the human heart.[16]

Moving on from Arendt a little, I want to take the opportunity of the Presocratics to ask the question why it appears to mean so much to us in the West that ancient should mean ancient and modern should mean modern. This is why at the start of this chapter I invoked the poet Walt Whitman and the idea of predestination. For I am greatly disturbed by how very much it does seem to matter to us that what we understand as linear time be measured, as I put it a little earlier, in 'increments of intellectual, cultural and technological advancement'. As though we were always climbing a mountain, and each step were bringing us closer to the summit. Within this metaphor, the Presocratics have been like an important and obvious base camp. As a base camp, they have represented the concentration of everything that went before them into a sudden and dramatic resolve to climb; though perhaps it is relevant to imagine that the preconditions had been there in the Western project for a while already, so that others before them might have realized their moment. But seize it they did, and at the time that they did; and ever since them, it has accordingly been to the Presocratics that we have returned if we have been exhausted from climbing; or if we needed new oxygen bottles and a reminder of why we had committed to climbing in the first place. For surely the point of reaching a summit is to be able to look down and see the base camp far below – then out beyond it and around it, and even more exhilarating, a whole lower altitude of life from which one has escaped, at last, by sheer hard critical thinking.

If the Presocratics were a number, let's say the number ten, we would probably like to think of ourselves as the number thirty. At number one would probably be a cave called Shanidar in Iraq, where 100 000 years ago Neanderthals lived, who seem to have buried their dead with simple flowers in an early gesture of human loving. At around number twenty-seven, we would expect to find Charles Darwin and his *On the Origin of Species*. So yes: you have to admit that this counted-out sense of achievement does matter very much to us. So much so that it is hardly ever itself singled out and talked about like this – hardly ever made the object of investigation, as indeed I hope to make it here, in this book.

When Francis Macdonald Cornford wrote his classic study of Presocratic thought – *From Religion to Philosophy: A Study in the Origins of Western Speculation* – he used this same system of counting out achievement. At the time when he first published his book, in 1912, this was a radical enough approach for him to take. Radical because his idea that Western speculation should be regarded as a continuum, with human behaviour as its underlying number system, was an idea that could very seriously threaten to rob Christian revelation of its special position over it all, and even make Christianity itself out to be just another item of study according to historical-critical methods. For example, to a Christian scholar like Charles Gore, writing in his 1929 Gifford Lectures, the traditional university subject of divinity was still to be regarded as the 'queen science' – soaring over the other disciplines and reconciling in Christ their relativisms and empiricisms and factionalisms.[17] Cornford's thesis, which was inspired by some of the leading Continental sociologists of his day, was, albeit incidentally, a brilliant and meticulous desacralization of this hallowed distinction.[18] And because his book was such a detailed and systematic outworking of his argument, it continues to influence how scholars approach the Presocratics to this day. There may now be lively discussions over how far the Presocratics can be called philosophers and scientists, or even whether they should be called theologians instead; but it remains that all of these positions have been made possible by Cornford's pioneering effort to 'tell the time' by the archaeological logics of *uti-frui*. From flowers at a Neanderthal burial site to the most up-to-the-minute naturalism, Cornford's way is still our way of working out what is 'really going on in the world'.[19] In academic circles at least, it is increasingly difficult to make the case that some facts should be raised in significance above others: in the manner, that is, as Christianity traditionally taught that Christ's supernatural resurrection from the dead should be raised to be the arch fact and sentinel of all final knowledge. Like Wordsworth's 'Aerial keystone haughtily secure'. Or in the Church father Tertullian's more provocative language from the second century A.D.:

> The Son of God was crucified; it is not shameful because it ought to cause shame. And the Son of God died; it is believable because it can't be grasped. And having been entombed, He arose; it is certain because it is impossible.[20]

Understanding, insofar as it is now to be based upon less paradoxical certainties, has become a more Presbyterian creed. And the Presocratics – because they are the number ten, with such portentous things either side of them – are still regarded as the pre-eminent test case of this.

The White Mind responds to the charge of Frantz Fanon by saying that all facts deserve an equal consideration, and that Western science is the arch-proof of this. So the foundational event called the 'birth of Western philosophy' must continue to undergo correcting and grading in this direction. The Presocratics must not be allowed to appear as prophets issuing revelation. Not Wordsworth, then, but much more something to the idea of Shakespeare's *Richard III*: 'Richard loves Richard; that is, I am I.' Their very own rationalizing methods must be turned back upon them, and thus the chair kicked out from under them, until they hang lifeless (so will be the effect) – their ideas and systems filiated to the Near Eastern esotericism on the one side of them, and on the other side, to the displays of practical wisdom and know-how, coterminous with what they were doing, though not recorded in the annals of the history of philosophy. As we shall in due time see, Thales, the first of the Presocratics, exemplifies this situation. He has gone down in history as the first philosopher; yet no small part of his achievement in his own time was in the fields of astronomy and what we would now call 'military engineering'. Both of those to be considered surely as demanding a use of his native intelligence as philosophy; and both therefore a serious challenge to the notion that what the Presocratics managed was evolutionary on behalf of all humankind.

Cannibalism

It is altogether an ironic state of affairs. The Western mind desires, on the one hand, to show that it was born legitimately to noble parents. Yet on the other hand, the more it returns in books and articles and tries to do just that and trace its roots, it discovers that the very critical faculties that are its birthright through the Presocratics are going to turn out to be the same things that threaten finally to destroy its legitimacy and specialness. What I mean is this: if the basis of what I earlier called the 'Presbyterian creed' is a belief in the democracy of facts, then the facts leading up to and away from the Presocratics will in the end only serve to show that nothing miraculous erupted or sprang into life with them. For does not the calm rational mind know that beneath such apparent dazzling on the surface – beneath such apparent innovation *ex nihilo* – is an inborn coding, always the same? 'Richard loves Richard; that is, I am I.' Deep, deep beneath cave paintings and myth and the first philosophy there lurks no mystical secret, but only some identical, irrepressible and agitating human agency. Call it what you like. Call it self-consciousness. Call it survivalism. Call it the thing that sets us apart from the beasts. But in the new secular Academy, please don't try to make out anymore that it has been like a series of appointments with destiny – 'Age after age until the arch of Christendom', to quote Wordsworth once again.

Here, for example, is part of Cornford's own explanation of what he set out to do in his classic study of the Presocratics:

> I shall try to prove that a real thread of continuity can be traced back from the final achievement of science – the representation of a world of individual atoms, governed by Necessity or Chance – to the final achievement of Olympianism, mirrored in Homer's

supernatural world of individual gods, subordinate to Destiny (*Moira*). This subjection of all individual powers, divine and human, to *Moira* is the profoundest, and (at first sight) the most baffling, dogma in this type of religion... in which it holds the place now occupied by Natural Law... [W]e seem able to make out that Philosophy, when she puts aside the finished products of religion and returns to the 'nature of things,' really goes back to that original representation out of which mythology itself had gathered shape. If we now call it 'metaphysical,' instead of 'supernatural,' the thing itself has not essentially changed its character. What has changed is, rather, man's attitude to it, which, from being active and emotional, has become intellectual and speculative. His earlier, emotional reaction gave birth to the symbols of myth, to objects of faith; his new procedure of critical analysis dissects it into concepts, from which it deduces various types of systematic theory.[21]

This was an extremely attractive and exciting discovery to have made. For prior to the sixth century B.C., and Thales as the first philosopher, there had occurred an event that is now unanimously referred to as the start of Western literature proper. This was in the eighth century B.C. with the epic poet Homer – and his poems the *Iliad* and the *Odyssey*. Roughly contemporaneous with Homer was Hesiod, another poet; one of whose poems, *Works and Days*, is possibly the first instance in Western literature of an author prepared to deliver his voice to the world with some style and premeditation. It was scripted as a letter of homespun advice to Hesiod's brother Perses. It contains many difficult to place but ultimately satisfying instructions like: 'Don't urinate whilst standing up and facing the sun.' It is, however, his other poem *Theogony*, which is more to the point here. It was composed to offer an account of the creation of the universe as well as of the genealogy of the gods. And along with Homer's epic poems, it belongs within the meaning of the intellectual scheme which Cornford was declaring to have discovered above – his 'final achievement of Olympianism'. Historically speaking, both poets were taking for their perspective a long, romantic look back from their own – eighth century B.C. – right the way back to the golden age of the Mycenaean civilization that had flourished many centuries before them. This golden age was to end abruptly and somewhat mysteriously around the twelfth century B.C. It was the age of the Greek victory in the Trojan War; and according to Homer at least, an aristocratic and chivalrous age in which both men and gods could be interpreted according to an overarching conception of moral duty – Cornford's *Moira*. When, towards the end of the *Odyssey*, Antinous lashes out and strikes Odysseus with a stool, he is reminded in no uncertain terms by one of his brave companions of this eternal slide rule:

> Antinous, you did wrong to strike the wretched vagabond. You're a doomed man if he turns out to be some god from heaven. And the gods do disguise themselves as strangers from abroad, and wander around our towns in every kind of shape to see whether people are behaving themselves or getting out of hand.[22]

I find, therefore, that I am broadly in line with Gilbert Murray when he wants to say that the Olympian system of religion, as we have to discover it today in a writer like Homer, that is as a world like Narnia rather than as a treatise or an encyclopaedia, is a reminder of the organizing power of sheer beauty. 'Truth, no doubt, is greater than beauty.' –

> But in many matters beauty can be attained and truth cannot. All we know is that when the best minds seek for truth the result is apt to be beautiful. It was a great thing that men should envisage the world as governed, not by Giants and Gorgons and dealers in eternal torture, but by some human and more than human Understanding, by beings of quiet splendour like many a classical Zeus and Hermes and Demeter. If Olympianism was not a religious faith, it was at least a vital force in the shaping of cities and societies which remain after two thousand years a type to the world of beauty and freedom and high endeavour. Even the stirring of its ashes, when they seemed long cold, had power to produce something of the same result; for the classicism of the Italian Renaissance is a child, however fallen, of the Olympian spirit.[23]

However, I want, over the next few pages, to add to this insight by noticing how this enduring influence of Homer's epic novel has been secured by a feature which it shares with all other writings that are admired if they too can hold up the mirror to human nature. Then I want to circle back to Cornford and his thesis and relate this feature to what Cornford calls there 'the final achievement of science – the representation of a world of individual atoms, governed by Necessity or Chance'.

When we read a novel like Homer's *Odyssey*, we take it for granted that there is a ready-written storyline: so that as we read our way through the pages, what we look for and enjoy (if indeed it is a book that is making us look and enjoy) is the relationship of truthfulness that strikes up between that storyline and the characters we are following through it as we read. The 'ready-written storyline' is of course a kind of Predestination, or Necessity or Chance; but what it does for us, the onlookers and readers, is to give us the opportunity to use that thing we use – call it an inner gyro – when we recognize and rate authentic human activity. Like when we recognize it on the page as much as in life. Not all writing would be good enough to activate this opportunity. But the very best of writing on the human condition seems to be what it is because it creates a perfect combination out of these two elements. The storyline, which when you think about it should be an outrage against the free and realistic movements of the characters (in time), becomes something that appears to spread out behind them, page by page; as indeed our life stories spread out behind us in real time like the wake cast from a ship. But by the same token, a human life without a storyline would seem an equally outrageous concept to us. Like we were just dry leaves blown this way and that. It is true that the very definition of free and self-determined action is to be making one's life up as one goes along, without any outside forces dictating it back to one. But it now appears to be true on top of this again that we yearn for some sensation of confession against the facts. We want to be carefree without a thought *and yet* culpable, and in the dock, and recounting how it was all so cleverly done.

In light of this, I find that I am not surprised at all by Cornford's discovery that the story-making of the birth of Western literature and the story-making of the birth of Western philosophy and science both required a vital element of Predestination. And that both their claims to truth and credibility required the establishment of a direct causal relationship between what was observed to be happening and what was really going on – whether the latter be on some cruel game-board played on high with the pieces of our lives, or underneath it all as trillions of teeming atoms, the pawns of some all-powerful mathematics.

However, all of this only makes me want to ask again the question that I asked after Arendt: 'Why should ancient mean ancient and modern mean modern?' Cornford says that once upon a time when Homer and Hesiod were writing, the attitude of the Western mind to life was predominately 'active and emotional'. This produced religion and myth and the epic. Then something changed, so that this attitude could advance to become 'intellectual and speculative'. First, though, a further word about Homer and Hesiod, so that this 'active and emotional' can be put in its proper context.

The story of Western literature, when it catches them, catches them in the act of regrouping and rebuilding after a comparative Dark Age that had already been some four centuries long. The Greeks were rising again: rising towards the discovery of the fifth century B.C. city and its civic and intellectual ideals, as perfected in Athens: and rising towards what would ever after be thought of as their shared sense of Hellenism and its lesson to the world. And as so often happens at these times when forward momentum looks for its reflection in the hand that has pushed it, the characters of Homer's tales were magnified into their greatness just as much as Hesiod's gods and goddesses were taken back to have fantastic beginnings in the elemental forces of the world.[24] It is as though Homer and Hesiod were trying to gather up and transmit to posterity the mythical and religious 'dream songs' of the Greek people. As I have already indicated, these dream songs were to include the materials of cosmogonies and theogonies; and given the traditionally mercantile nature of Greek life around the Mediterranean, they were also to exhibit a good amount of intriguing cross-fertilization with the dream songs of nearby civilizations like the Egyptian, Hittite and Babylonian. Consider the imagination at work in the following example from Hesiod's *Theogony*:

> And Night bare hateful Doom and black Fate and Death, and she bare Sleep and the tribe of Dreams. And again the goddess murky Night, though she lay with none, bare Blame and painful Woe, and the Hesperides who guard the rich, golden apples and the trees bearing fruit beyond glorious Ocean. Also she bare the Destinies and ruthless avenging Fates, Clotho and Lachesis and Atropos, who give men at their birth both evil and good to have, and they pursue the transgressions of men and of gods: and these goddesses never cease from their dread anger until they punish

the sinner with a sore penalty. Also deadly Night bare Nemesis (Indignation) to afflict mortal men, and after her, Deceit and Friendship and hateful Age and hard-hearted Strife.[25]

If we zoom out now and jump through the Presocratics to Thucydides' account of Pericles' iconic 'Funeral Speech', we get to see how the glory of Athens and a post-philosophical climate had already conspired to render a little embarrassing this sort of thing. To return to an earlier metaphor, the tribe in the jungle that protects itself by being hostile to strangers and jealously guarding its dream songs is felt by Western eyes to be factional, and a step short of the universal humanism that would render such primitive hoarding unnecessary. Pericles' 'Funeral Speech' remains so iconic today because it truly does read as the prototype manifesto against this primitivism – it still provides our best rationale for why it must be rounded up, and rounded on, in the end. Of course it might be said in defence at this point that the West no longer practices such vigorous colonialisms: and that its study of brown people in the jungle is now carried on as a respectfully neutral discipline: and all in the name of an innocent wonder. However, by going back to Pericles we can recover a different, more muscular perspective on it all. And yes, I want to draw attention to it because it is the challenge to my question why ancient and modern should always have to stand in attitudes of suspicion to one another. And why that suspicion should have such power to order the generations of humankind into their lines, almost without murmur of sedition or dissent.

Pericles takes the step, unusual at the time, of proclaiming his Athens to be an 'open access society'. Today, we in the West have the advantage of knowing exactly what he means by this because we actually live in societies that believe themselves to be in the direct line of this. Pericles says,

> We lay our city open to all, and at no time evict or keep the stranger away from the knowledge or sight of anything which it might help an enemy to see revealed. Our belief is not primarily in munitions and concealment, but in our spirit in action. In forms of training, too, our adversaries strive for valour in laboured practice from their childhood up, while we live our life unregimented, yet we go to meet danger as great as theirs.[26]

It is almost as though this were compiled as a document of the Cold War. The imputation against munitions and concealment could fit into the discourse of the Bay of Pigs episode; while the distaste for adversaries who 'strive for valour in laboured practice from their childhood up' reads like an indictment of the East German sports programme. What stands against these things in Pericles' statement is 'our spirit in action'. Here, the veneration of his speech within Western ideas becomes clear: because what could be a better transcription of the democratic ideal of freedom than this? The human spirit in action is a value and virtue for a universe of humans. As an idea, it is therefore intrinsically superior to the idea of the tribe, with its (outwardly at least) arbitrary and accidental customs. It is for this reason more than just an idea. It is a fully provisioned outlook on human affairs. It is, as I have been suggesting, a theory of time as well as a theory of education, where theories of time and education can very quickly degenerate into theories of racial and intellectual superiority – though that particular stone is not one that I plan to turn in this book. It should, however, come as no surprise to see that a little later on in his speech, Pericles rounds defiantly on his past:

> We have no further need of a Homer to praise us, or any other poet whose words give transient pleasure, but the real truth will discredit their account.[27]

For his point is that, in the open access society, the data and metadata of the human condition, when laid bare by reason, and the better to debunk every superstition and dream song, does a curious thing in addition to this. In order to get at and unleash the full force of the 'spirit in action', it produces a declaration of rights as an important and necessary step. As an important and necessary step in the direction of impartiality, sentiment and civilization – for remember, the tribe in the jungle might kill and eat a stranger just for being a stranger. Clearly this is intolerable. Therefore, the declaration of rights, when it comes, targets this savagery with an appeal to the intellectual brotherhood of man. It says that the data and metadata of the human condition, like human biology and modern medicine, is a discovery of equal application and worth to all. The question and challenge for all human beings everywhere becomes then to bring themselves out from their tunnel vision and savagery, and into the World-Mind that comprehends that to be as irreproachably good as this is what is in its best and final interests.[28]

When the rocketry and space pioneer Dr Wernher von Braun escaped from a falling Nazi Germany and made it to America, he was freed from the constriction of having to build V2 terror rockets and released wholesale into the general service of the human species. His public summation of the staggering Apollo XI mission to the moon stands now as a perfect testimony to the phenomenon I am trying to highlight. Where what I mean by the phenomenon is not rockets or spaceships or any other such stunning things, but the speech patterns they coax from our lips – and how these speech patterns seem to talk through these corporeal objects of their initial focus and out beyond them to an otherworldly audience of *One*. Just *Who* is the human race trying to impress with these speech patterns? For they are always the same, always summoned up and aired at our greatest moments. I could not, for instance, think of a straighter line between Pericles' vision of 'our spirit in action' and this from von Braun:

> It has created names and dates that will be recorded in history for thousands of years. And that has expanded man's mind and caused a new wave of thought to sweep across the earth. For the first time, life has left its planetary cradle and the ultimate destiny of man is no longer confined to the earth. I hope now that these brave Apollo eleven astronauts can be assured that their trip was not in vain, that our reach into space will be continued and that from their brief journey of exploration there will be a brighter future for mankind.[29]

Now, such straight lines as this, when they leap across two thousand and more years of history, do a particular and peculiar thing. They dehumanize the human. That is to say, in the name of the ultimate progress and survival of the species (because one would never do it otherwise), they dehumanize the human. They take the soul out of the human animal. We all know what I mean by this. And furthermore, we all know that *what* I mean by this is what I mean to achieve by my insistent questioning of why the concepts of ancient and modern should peg us all out like long-dead exhibits in a museum display (of evolution).

Western rationality, Western science and Western philosophy only work because the human body upon which they work is already dead. Because of course it has to be dead if the predestinated destinations of its physiological processes, its atoms and noxious gases, are to retain their integrity and be reached by its certain decay before our eyes. This is the same thing as to say that trainee doctors work on cadavers, while priests, artists and shamans work on the living soul. This work on the living soul already assumes that ancient and modern do not mean what the Western mind thinks that they should mean. In fact it assumes that there is a perspective from which they need not mean anything at all. This is the perspective exemplified in Walt Whitman's poem 'I Sing the Body Electric' (and we have got there at last). Those like Whitman who cannot bear to see the soul and the body separated under a forensic reason, on tabletops of cold stainless steel, want to see instead a timeless and eternal succession of personalities. A succession of human beings so special and distinct from each other that the soul, in effect, becomes the body – and by becoming the body, violates the dispassion and impersonalism (the Hippocratic oath) that makes the Western mind as brilliant and as efficient as it assuredly is. This statement of mine is really a statement, then, about what access-routes to the Real we may have, and about forms of knowledge and their contents.

Whitman says that one supremely important access-route to the Real is what we see plain face in the mirror, and then in other people we look at. We do not see the soul because that is invisible. So we see the body. But we do not see the body as our cold, unblooded reason can be educated to see it. We see it in a loving, lustful way as recognizable and evocative and unique as a scent:

> O my body! I dare not desert the likes of you in other men/and women, nor the likes of the parts of you,/I believe the likes of you are to stand or fall with the likes/of the soul, (and that they are the soul,)[30]

One of the staples of Western philosophy ever since the Presocratics has been the opposite of this: that the mind should rise above the body and its heats and rule it bird's-eye fashion from above. The mind should learn to see the bigger picture; first the bigger picture of 'proper' self-love and dignity; and then the bigger picture of the human race – its survival above all else, and its eventual occupancy of other planets than this blue one, if survival comes to mean that one day. This essential dualism of the 'spirit in action' is hardly ever questioned. But now I want to question it in this book; and I want to see in the end where it takes us. Because there seems to me to be a paradox and an irony at work in this scheme, as admirable and commonsensical as it is meant to be. It is as though we are all of us leading versions of posthumous lives, but over just a *single*, sacramental body on its tabletop of cold stainless steel – and just a single body, because, as per Plato's analogy of the cave, everything else is just opinion and shadows on the wall. There is nothing about individuality and subjectivity that you can learn and notate. They are experiences to be had by people at large. They are what humans were made to communicate to each other. But when we talk about objective truth, we talk about a body of knowledge; and yes we mean just a single body of knowledge if we mean for truth to be incontrovertible and sacrosanct. And I hope it is clear from my illustration how our processes of ratiocination simply cannot cope with anything more than this, its discrete, atomic, nuclear knowledge. The Body. And yet we are bodies.

The child who learns to count, and the mathematical paradigm of truth, grows up to become the intellectual and the glacial eye. In its estimation of its own position in the timeline, this glacial eye is secure and unblinking. It looks back to antiquity and sees mistake after mistake. But it is also a good and magnanimous eye. It is not going to napalm all that error and impulsiveness it sees but write instead its interesting and tolerating histories of it. But the tragedy every time is that as we grow up into becoming wise and cool and all out of body like this, the body that we look back down on – all that knowledge – just can't any longer be as recognizable and unique and evocative as a scent. It just can't because it is no longer ours. It is *Gray's Anatomy* (where the Presocratics only had an inkling of it). In fact, the effect is that we were no longer having a life of our own at all any longer, but were simply contributing our stage of evolution to the corporate life of a single man, stretched out across the ages in some ghastly lonely dance. A single man sparked into dancing by the potential difference between ancient and modern – ever widening, ever more manic. But I cannot put it better than Blaise Pascal in his *Pensées*:

The whole succession of human beings throughout the course of the ages must be regarded as a single man, continually living and learning; and this shows how unwarranted is the deference we yield to the philosophers of antiquity; for, as old age is most distant from infancy, it must be manifest to all that old age in the universal man must be sought, not in the times nearest his birth, but in the times most distant from it. Those whom we call the ancients are really those who lived in the youth of the world, and the true infancy of man; and as we have added the experience of the ages between us and them to what they knew, it is only in ourselves that is to be found that antiquity which we venerate in others.[31]

So how would things look, then, if suddenly ancient and modern didn't have to mean the things that they do? What if it were possible to write about the Presocratic philosophers without this heavy Predestination hanging over us? I have talked about the number system of how we tell the time in these things. Let me now add this.

The point about a number system is that you can look up and down its length and make proof-perfect predictions about what goes where, what comes next, what came at early stages and so on. So I believe that it is disingenuous to talk about a 'history of philosophy' or a 'history of ideas', if by the content of these we mean a series of discoveries made like minerals from the ground, or fish from the sea. Because of course the history that we mean to imply is not some taxidermist's display of these things. It is much more like Giambattista Vico's *The New Science*. Even if not a scrap of evidence of the Presocratics had survived, we would still have been able to write them in as the missing link. That is, if we were good scientists we would have been able to do this (and what other kind of good is there, really?).

Here is the supreme wonder and irony of the Western mind as it is now. Scientific method vindicates itself by saying that the evidence came first, and that it only followed it obediently to its conclusions. The apple hit Newton on the head, and Darwin met the Fuegians. But the theories of gravity and evolution are not taught today as mere items of interest. Nor, for that matter, are the Presocratics taught like a group of Greek vases. All these seminal discoveries and discoverers are taught like a charge sheet levelled at the human race along its entire length. They are taught as though the history of Western philosophy has existed before all merely 'human time' – as though it has existed as the story of the most holy physics of the universe. They tell us that the history of Western philosophy has really been like a reward, a medal and an honour – pinned to the breasts of the heroes of the people. And I mean, of course, of the people of the whole earth. The stigma attaching to those who haven't earned its reward is the stigma of the white man's burden. It still is. Except we no longer describe backwardness in racial and intellectual terms but in economic terms. They are the undeveloped of the earth; and their backwardness is not their fault, which allows us to work to alleviate it with consciences held high, more vindicated than ever we could be when it was all about physical measurements and the thickness of people's skulls. And I haven't even mentioned the position of women in all of this yet. But don't worry I shall, just not here; not yet. In the final chapter, I shall do it. And I shall explore the extent to which there is male and female in the Western intellectual tradition. And I will have something to say about why it has to be male and female, and some mysterious mixture of the two, and not the sexless reason of a supercomputer and data, metadata and meta-metadata.

A real romance

So what I am really saying here is this: you can't have it both ways: you can't logically talk about science as the paradigm of truthfulness and right reason, because you believe it to be the same thing as the lawful way of the universe, then turn around and talk like it has been a series of human discoveries. You can't form a scathing opinion of religion and the soul, then point to an apple in a tree to prove your point. The apple may very well be in the tree and the religionist you are attempting to debunk may have no such ready way to point to his God, but you have proved nothing. Or at least, you have not proved what you think you have proved. You may think that the apple and its falling prove gravity and energy, and that these things and others like them are the real forces at work in the universe. But deep in its bunker, real Science must surely know that gravity and energy are just names of the same order and function as the names of invisible things such as love, soul and God. There is nothing that the religionist can point to that proves love, soul and God. He may point to his wife to prove love, to his child to prove soul and to his Church to prove God. But don't for one second imagine that he is doing anything less than you who point at falling apples to prove gravity and energy. In both cases, he and you form words for things you cannot see; and that makes you just as bad as each other. For in all of these cases, what follows the words is a theory that tries to explain them. But the theories are expansive and discursive and contested, which indicates that they are never the same as the words, which pretended to precision. And for their part, the words were formed in the absence of being able to pin down and see the thing itself which they pointed to.

When a methodical realist like Thomas Hobbes admonished Scholastic metaphysics, it was with the glee of having realized that it had been using the language of visible things for the invisible. A dangerous gaffe in his opinion, and the error of what he termed 'separated essences' in tribute to its originator, Aristotle. He replaced it with a scheme by which words might merely signify the impressions made upon our senses by realities sufficient to make those impressions. He meant material realities.[32] But I am saying that all the things we select to be the things that shall matter to us become invisible things in that moment of their selection. Because the moment of their selection makes them things that we are romancing, not studying. You can romance the wrong things and have a strange romance, and you can romance the right things and have a real romance. But you cannot escape the fact that all human word-formation is initiated as a romance. All human words are therefore the words of invisible things. Because romance is of the order of invisible things. The efforts that Hobbes and others have made to overcome this problem by various degrees of sterilization are false victories. It is not the case that words and communication are the 'neutral' that we then contaminate with our 'partial'. It is the other way round. Words and ideas and theories are the endearing human weakness. The sum of all things is a creature that doesn't need to speak like we need to speak.

So why do we insist that our romances must compete with each other? I suppose it is down to human nature and power, and wanting to be first across the line. I also feel that I have set out enough already to be able to call it the fallacy of 'ancient and modern'. For example, the modern West points to the Presocratics and says, 'There is our apple!' 'There is philosophy, reason, truth!' And the rest of the world looks puzzled and is disturbed by this mean-spirited religion of the good life. And it asks, instead, 'Why do you point to mere men as though they could mean these things?' 'Only God could be pointed to by these mighty word-signs.' And then: 'Why does it mean so much to you anyway to plant your flag and claim such things for yourself?' 'Surely you realize that a man who so stakes his fortunes to such things loses, at once, the splendid originality of his life – like if he pointed to the soaring eagle and said, "there are thermals and aerodynamics".' 'You must learn to love and share the likeness of you in other men and women.' 'This is how you can be returned from the eternity of your imagination back into time; and into living in time again according to a real romance that does not betray you.'

This is what is so exciting and unusual about the Presocratics, but what has sadly also been so unsung about them. Because we are proud and want to be able to have a system of telling the time that positions us at the latest greatest hour, we went looking for the first philosophers – just like palaeontologists go looking today for that sublime event horizon between pre-human and human life. The Presocratics never had a hope of escaping. And according to the same logic, neither do we. Right now, in some unimagined future, we are being written about in the same way that we write about them. We would say that we are just getting on with the business of life (like they would have said) – uncertain amidst our hopes and fears and asking, 'Dear Diary what is it all about?' But right now, in some unimagined future and its page, we have ceased to exist as individuals and originalities at all. Little do we know it, but we are living through some 'moment' that is being written up and studied. Perhaps it is the birth of something, or its decline. Who can know – who ever knew the exact coordinates of what they were living through? Predestination, when it is enhanced like this by reason and science, is disturbingly complete. But mercifully, there is a way of fighting back! It begins by contrasting all of this with how it is that we actually live our lives as 'individuals and originalities'. I mean the contrast between what Virginia Woolf called 'the facts of history, of law, of biography' and what she called 'the still hidden facts of our still unknown psychology'.[33]

Perhaps this contrast is best depicted as a curiosity. This curiosity is that none of us chooses on a daily basis to live as though arbitrary factors such as where we were born and into what state of privilege were determining our future like geologic certainty. Yet when it comes to looking across at someone else's life – to reading a biography, or even writing one – this is the very logic we so casually and habitually impose as the very archetype of understanding itself. 'Our subject was born in such and such a country, so that must explain this and that theme in his work', and everyone nods their heads in sage agreement. Anything to do with sexuality would, of course, be absolute gold dust, and the 'a-ha' moment, and explain everything. I would like to add that in today's world, where we like to think that we have worked so hard towards equality and fairness, this prurient way of operating becomes more curious a cruelty still.

No, how we actually live our lives is from the soul outwards, radiating history-destroying death rays from our every freeborn decision. We can dream: and it must mean something to dream. Why, when we can have such definite critical perspectives on whole sweeps of history and historical personalities (and the next-door neighbours), can we still go home at night and be such a total mystery to ourselves? 'Dear Diary, what should I do with my life... ?' The only answer must be in what causes this contrast: and clearly I believe that this is the soul. And clearly I believe, finally, that a new history that works in this way also, from the inside of the soul outwards, can begin to achieve our breakout from the sickly sweet saintliness, and international conspiracy, of judging and historicizing others into oblivion. Because it is not actually what we want, or are even best at (and that is why I can talk of an international conspiracy and hypocrisy). What we want and are best at is the loving, generous, empathy that it is the intrinsically human quality to give. We do this magnificent thing all the time without thinking about it, but when it comes to being intellectual, we knit our brows and it all slows up, and nothing is effortless anymore but hard problems to solve; so I have seriously begun to consider whether these problems are of our own making – and that the way forward will therefore be to go back to where it all started and give ourselves a chance to just start being nice and respectful to everyone and everything again. To start treating the intellectual histories of things in the *possessive* way that we already treat our families and friends – on their side before they have even opened their mouths, and as biased, and prejudiced, and as unequal as we are entitled to be to the objects of our love.

2

The Way of Truth

I can only describe my feeling by the metaphor, that, if a man could write a book on Ethics which really was a book on Ethics, this book would, with an explosion, destroy all the other books in the world.

LUDWIG WITTGENSTEIN

The situation that I have been describing in the previous chapter is like a parable. You are born into this world – and always, it must be said, through no choice of your own. As soon as you are old enough to act on the information, you are invited by your elders and betters to consider the fact that what you thought was the world is not really the world at all. Perhaps you were blessed with a particularly strong imagination and have been voyaging with success in the land of Make-Believe. Now you will gently be induced to mistrust your land and its foundations. If your elders and betters are kind and sympathetic, they will let this take a gradual course. Where once your land of Make-Believe was simply humoured or ignored, you will now be introduced to the sensation that it is being actively tolerated. This will also be your first lesson in magnanimity. Notice how they smile at you. If you are lucky you will one day get to see this smile in operation in its natural habitat – in its helicopter over that jungle full of brown faces.

For that smile and that toleration have been carefully calculated to develop in you a state of mild paranoia, though you will only ever hear it talked about in its positive spin, as 'wonder'. Thus gets under way a structured cruelty that you will one day get to inflict on the next generation in their turn – if it can first succeed on you. Why did I just say 'cruelty'? I said that word because in your land of Make-Believe, you were king and creator of all you surveyed. You had no 'wonder' because you had no sense of enervation and insufficiency. It was only with that smile and its toleration that you began to suspect that you had been labouring under misapprehensions; and that what is called 'the world' was not your world of the imagination at all, but really what you had been noticing adults talk about, conspiratorially, under the banner of *realism*. Because realism vindicates wonder. If wonder is like a door you open into a new world, then realism is that world. And realism has to be that world because of course no one as selfish and risk-averse as an adult human would ever risk opening the door on a world that they hadn't already predicted a fair bit about. By the way, that prudent attitude of the mind also is realism. Yes: realism stitches up both sides of the equation and is supremely disappointing in the end for this reason. It is logically impossible to have a proper, surprising realist adventure. Realism is much more likely to bring you to the point of saying 'I told you so' to someone. I have used words like 'cruelty' and 'disappointing', but of course nothing to do with realism need necessarily be a bad thing. Realism makes the trains run on time and the world go round and keeps us as much as possible out of harm's way. Who doesn't want that? Who doesn't want to eradicate as far as possible the hit-and-miss thrills of the imagination and conform as closely as they can to traffic regulations and the rules of health and hygiene?

This is why we batter children with *realism* from the moment they can be ruled responsible for taking it in. And this is why we never look back to take seriously what came first for them. I mean by this that whole world of Make-Believe which was a whole and complete world before we scoffed it off. A whole and complete world shot through with truths and mysteries of its own – with these truths and mysteries representing the only bulwark against the international conspiracy and hypocrisy of realism that there can be. Which is why I spent the whole preceding chapter laying out a vision of the ancient and modern, and how it is that we see such towering good sense in calculating all our living and thinking in multiples of modern versus ancient.

A land called Make-Believe

So it was once that you were a child, king and creator of an ancient land called Make-Believe, untroubled by the modern, adult paranoia about such things. Although I should admit that 'paranoia' is a harsh word used here principally for effect. For if realism is, at any moment on earth, the facts of the matter, then adults are entitled and morally obligated to instruct children in the ways of the world and crossing the road. But in a book like this which purports to report on every available nuance left in the old story of the birth of Western philosophy, this *omertà* has to be broken.

It has to be broken because the parable is, for sure, the description of an *omertà* – of the consequences of speaking out. In your land of Make-Believe, you wielded enormous and exceptional powers. You were free to make up characters, human characters; but not only human characters; you were free also to irradiate non-human, animal characters with the personalities of humans. Even to do the same to inanimate objects. And it felt good to do this, it felt right. More than right, it felt dignified. More than dignified, it felt spiritually and emotionally fulfilling. Before the adults crashed in and taught utility to you – that your equipment will be judged on what it was ultimately applied to – you felt spiritual and emotional fulfilment in your power to project onto whatever you should wish those beautiful, moving, human qualities. These projected qualities were your way of being in a world and sensing your interrelatedness to its parts and processes – but here is the crucial difference, of instating your debt and duty to all of this interrelatedness at the same time. That and that only was your freedom. Your freedom was an onomastic freedom. Your freedom was to take an unbending, glacial world and soften it and humanize it with names and possessiveness – to make it yours and yours alone. And it wasn't just you projecting all the time: you definitely felt something coming back. You actually tangibly felt the gratefulness of a world returning its love to you. Not just your pet dog, but all of it: every sunrise and every sunset. Every mountain and every river. You felt that all of these things that wouldn't otherwise have had names or voices or identities became grateful to you and loved you because of this massive freely given thing that you had done for them.

Did you ever look around you when you were doing this? Did you ever look at how it goes in the world of adults? Just take a look now. Let's take a look at how adults treat this blue planet. Let's look at how they dam and choke those rivers for electricity. Let's look at how they punch tunnels through the mountains and mine them for minerals. What about the animals? They have been caged and experimented on and sent into orbit to die of heat exhaustion in the name of interplanetary travel. I haven't even had to mention the unspeakable things that adults are willing to do to themselves and each other in wars and other crimes. All of these atrocities are supported in some way or other by realism. The exploitation of the natural world, its minerals and animals is supported by the survivalist imperative of the material needs of life. The unspeakable crimes of the adult condition are supported by (or rather they do support) the realist description of human nature as essentially self-serving. While the sexual imperative to dominate lands as much as bodies may well be what the survivalist instinct does boil down to in the end.

However, perhaps I go too far with all of this – perhaps I am judging the world of adults from the point of view of a utopia that has never existed? Perhaps I am overstating the traumas of childhood: that is to say, the traumas of childhood as they are stoked and aggravated by the need to grow up. Surely it must be an intrinsically good thing to develop and broaden into becoming a fully paid-up member of the world of adults? Surely if you start out life as 'ancient', you must want to end it as 'modern'? More damning still, I suppose, would be to point out to me that childhood, like the infancy of the Western mind or the jungle full of brown faces, doesn't in fact have any of the existence and credibility that I am attributing to it. Childhood, like the infancy of the Western mind or the jungle full of brown faces, are things that are to be smiled at and tolerated because they are nowadays so completely documented and understood by the international adult Academy. On this argument, no child ever went through the experience that I am describing. What they went through, in fact, were various classifiable episodes, corresponding exactly to what science has learnt of the stages of human maturation. There never was any world of Make-Believe that could stand on its own against this level of analysis. Just like there never was any first philosophy or primitive culture that could stand its analysis by our present state of intelligence. This is how it always goes: modern always destroys ancient for good and forever. There is no comeback, or fight back, for ancient. There are, of course, recurring bouts of sentiment for an original, organic, classic earthiness in life. For food miles and the home-baked. But remember that sentiment can only be sentiment by arising from *within* a system. Sentiment, therefore, is one of the staunchest supporters of the system. It is no revolutionary. It is just how we mark time until realism's next purge. An energy crisis, a state of martial law, an economic collapse – all of these events, and others, would kick sentiment into touch.

Two quick examples now from history that offer pauses for thought in various directions on the theme of 'purge'. The first is the possibly apocryphal story of Alexander the Great and the pirate. At some time, a notorious pirate was supposedly caught red-handed and brought before Alexander for amusement – before what would then have been his judgement and execution. Alexander said to the pirate something like: 'Now have your chance and tell us what you mean by infesting the seas like this!' And the pirate is alleged to have answered along the lines of: 'Well, I tell you then: just the same thing that you mean by infesting the world. Except that I do it in a little ship and for that restriction am called a pirate, and you do it with a whole fleet, and by sheer dint of force and number are called an Emperor.' It is alleged that this story was known to the ancient world from a now lost passage in Cicero's *De re publica*, Book III. The medieval churchman and political theorist John of Salisbury produced an even fuller version of this story in his *Policraticus*. And even a name for the pirate: Dionides. This is what he has him saying in his version:

> If Alexander were alone and should be taken, he would be a pirate. If the people hung upon the nod of Dionides, Dionides would be emperor. As a matter of right there is no difference between us except that he is the worse who is the more ruthless in plundering, the more contemptible in disregarding justice, and the more brazen in disregard for laws. These I flee, but you wage wars against them; I have a degree of respect for them; you flout them. It is bad luck and financial difficulties that have made me a thief; it is intolerable pride and insatiate greed that have made the same of you. Should fortune smile perhaps I would become a better man, but with you the more fortunate you are, the worse you will become![1]

Likewise, Diodorus Siculus has preserved in his *Bibliotecha historica* the story of what Philomelus did, when, as commander of the Phocian League, he attacked Delphi and commandeered the oracle:

> When Philomelus had control of the oracle he directed the Pythia to make her prophecies from the tripod in the ancestral fashion. But when she replied that such was not the ancestral fashion, he threatened her harshly and compelled her to mount the tripod. Then when she frankly declared, referring to the superior power of the man who was resorting to violence: 'It is in your power to do as you please,' he gladly accepted her utterance and declared that he had the oracle which suited him.[2]

Perhaps it would go better if I explained what I mean like this: The Western mind says,

> I have no prehistory, I have no infancy, I have no Make-Believe. I have always been there as the best that you could be as a human being. I was your best ideas and your best interests. I have never changed. It is *you* who have changed. It is *you* who have borne the stigmas and excitements of coming into the understanding of this. There has never been a history of happenstance independent of me. What is called history has been a consequence of *your* fallibility, because I am infallible and I am eternal. This means, too, that history will not go on forever. History will be extinguished when the line of wet sticky humans dries up for good. History will end with something called *The Last White Man* – for this is the real meaning of the burden which I believe I have had to carry on behalf of everyone else. I will continue to work tirelessly to convert every human being into a single *White Man* because all the partialities of colour and sex must be reversed until Reason can operate endlessly and unencumbered, in the form of a single, corporate being. Then, when that wondrous day has been reached, this *Last White Man* must be destroyed – must sacrifice himself in the name of colourless, sexless, odourless Truth.

I ask in response: Is this what we want? Or do we rather want to fight and scrap for something less convergent and more reckless like Whitman's vision of *The Body Electric*?

I mentioned Plato's famous 'analogy of the cave' in Chapter 1; and now I want to bring it out once again to put an intellectual and chronological fix on what I am talking about here. I want to do this because Plato's analogy of the cave is such a simple and powerful depiction of the Socratic ideal and of its continuing hold over the Western consciousness. And it explains how it achieves this hold by singling out and holding aloft the fault line and trauma of the ancient, the parochial, the darkness, the cave. It says that the dividing line, and all that matters, is between those that huddle together around opinions and ghosting shadows and those that have been gifted with the talent to leave the huddle and walk out into the light. Whereas I want to say that there is no overarching bigger picture like this, but that the fault lines that really matter are as numerous and idiosyncratic as the originality of each life that springs into being, which leaves it that the trauma upon which Socrates and the story of Western philosophy really hangs is the trauma of how childhood innocence is levelled and graded into the single path and journey of *The Last White Man*.

In Plato's *Republic*, the analogy of the cave comes about because Socrates is challenged to define what he means by the 'Form of the Good' as the ultimate object of the philosopher's desire for wisdom. What Socrates and Plato mean by the Form of the Good, I have here been referencing in my imagery of the 'Western Mind', its colourless, sexless, odourless self.

For Socrates and his disciple and biographer Plato, the point of leverage that philosophy takes again and again to the world of human life is the difference that can be recognized at any time between mere dream-state and opinion-forming and the superiority of what they call 'pure-form' knowledge. I say 'superiority' because for Socrates and Plato, our ordinary relationship to knowledge is experienced as a particularly nasty kind of embarrassment – embarrassment as we writhe, *in flagrante*, in the distance measured out between the eyes-wide-open enjoyment of life and the eye-in-the-sky. Understand that for Socrates and Plato, the future really does exist in some perfect setting of the perfect forms of all encountered reality: and because it exists like this, it can function also like this eternal scolding I am describing. We can never catch up with it. Of course, the very idea of the past catching up with the future is ridiculous and can never happen, but that is not really their point. Or perhaps they don't quite see it in that way. Perhaps if you think of the future impersonally, as *knowledge*, rather than personally, as *God*, then you don't get mad like people get mad at God over Predestination. In the *Republic*, Plato has a very specific way of describing his future of knowledge. Or what is the same thing, his vision of a pristine understanding that would gift the God-like vision, if only we could attain to it.

Imagine the best that we can normally do, he says; this will be the kind of understanding that we get through geometry and other subjects that also work from first principles and hypotheses. First principles and hypotheses can be mesmerizing and inspiring, especially when they lead us out onto the cosmic patterns of life. But just imagine now if these truths could themselves become the objects of our intellection, so that through them we could see and reach into another dimension altogether. Who could want more from their truth than the safe knowledge that 1 + 1 will always = 2? But just imagine now if knowledge-situations like this were merely the portals to something infinitely better. I have described its effect as like being able to see the future: but on Plato's description from Book VI of the *Republic*, it almost sounds superior to that:

> This is the realm that reason masters with the power of dialectic. Assumptions are not treated as first principles but as real hypotheses. That is, they are not employed as beginnings but as ladders and springboards, used in order to reach that realm that requires no hypotheses and is therefore the true starting point for the attainment of unobstructed knowledge. When reason attains that level and becomes aware of the whole intelligible order, it descends at will to the level of conclusions but without the aid of sense objects. It reasons only by using forms. It moves from forms through forms to forms. And it completes its journey in forms.[3]

This reasoning explains why pure-form knowledge looks like the future in relation to sense-object knowledge which looks like the past. For example, if your understanding is dependent on the impressions that sense objects can make upon your mind, then you are stuck in the throes of everything that I have in fact been lauding thus far in the name of 'possessiveness'. You need to be able to happen upon things one by one; and a good deal of what you call fondness and familiarity depends upon the accident at work in this. Your home is where you just happened to grow up. Your mother tongue is an extension of that. And one could go on. To live in time like this is a beautiful thing. It makes love possible – once again, let me stress, because love needs you to be able to happen upon something and fix your emotions on it. We say to the one we love: 'You are the one and only'. The truth is that this is something that you could never say from the perspective of pure-form knowledge. You could never say it because you would be knowing all along that the one you love is not really the 'one and only'. Pure-form knowledge would make it impossible for you to escape from the truth that she was merely the one who you *happened* upon one fine day. Within you was the capacity to ascribe to her all the highest of high things, and you went on and did that – and the rest, as they say, is history. But if you could see the future in terms of knowledge, then something like this could never take place. There could be no projecting of emotions from some place of make-believe inside of you. There could be no story. There could be no love.

In Socrates' and Plato's analogy of the cave, these problems are not supposed. Human life is not treated as an originality that starts and ends with each new soul born into the world. The projection of emotions as possessiveness is not taken to signify a real and dignified world, begun with the beginning of each of us, and then destroyed on the order of the pretensions of 'objective truth'. In the analogy of the cave, it is called darkness in order that everything that is opposite to it – in order that objective truth – may be called light. This breathtaking move is meant to stand to reason and be the minimum standard for the proper conduct of human life. But I wonder that it may just be what I have called it, a breathtaking move; and I wonder that like many other breathtaking moves, it may be as wrong as it is right. On the one hand, it is certainly the case that objective truth means something important to us, otherwise Socrates and Plato wouldn't have had it as their move to make. But on the other hand, that doesn't then have to validate the move. And worse still, the move may have put us on the wrong side of a whole kind of knowledge, and a whole kind of seeing, these last 2500 years.

It is obvious that when we commit the mental act of differentiation, we place ourselves in a judge's seat the likes of which could never actually be encountered on earth, in time. Now because this transposition does definitely happen every time we differentiate, Socrates and Plato are entitled to say that it is a real process – are entitled to say that the ideas produced by differentiation are real and independent of us and possibly stand for a world that we could strive to enter and never leave. The World of the Forms. However, what seems to get left behind each time this logic is prosecuted is the question whether this would be a preferable world to the world we already inhabit. I mean a preferable world to us humans. It is this question that I am going into in this book of mine by arguing for the tearing down of ancient and modern. Socrates and Plato say,

> Now if a man believes in the existence of beautiful things, but not of Beauty itself, and cannot follow a guide who would lead him to a knowledge of it, is he not living in a dream? Consider: does not dreaming, whether one is awake or asleep, consist in mistaking a semblance for the reality it resembles?
> I should certainly call that dreaming. [Glaucon]
> Contrast with him the man who holds that there is such a thing as Beauty itself and can discern that essence as well as the things that partake of its character, without ever confusing the one with the other – is he a dreamer or living in a waking state?
> He is very much awake. [Glaucon][4]

Against them I say: Can Beauty itself exist in this way as Light imagined in deduction from the Darkness? Don't you have to shut your eyes in order to do this – in order to do any kind of mental deduction? Isn't that a terrible irony on the distinction that they would like to make between dreaming and waking? Everything in their argument and outlook hinges on Beauty itself being more real than the discrete things that we see and call beautiful; and certainly it is true that we find it easy to call many diverse things beautiful, which would suggest that it is not the diversity which we are naming when we do this but the abiding Beautiful itself. And I give that to them.

An explosion

But I (choose to) say again: What if what they would call the insuperable logic in this is really just another example of the religious impulse? What if the whole Good Life that they go on to derive from it is just that: another religion, with religion's desire to cheat and downgrade us out of our real knowledge and power – our real knowledge and power of understanding that we hold a serious and potent magic in our ability to name things. It seems far more likely and logical to me that when we project from our soul outwards the name of 'beautiful' onto something, we achieve by it not a homogenization, but an explosion. We explode the concept of objectivity, even though objectivity may exist in exactly the way that science seems to prove that it exists. Fire can be understood as a chemical process, following laws of nature. This kind of objectivity allows us to deduce correctly that to put our hand into the fire will each time burn us. But there is no relationship between this and what we do when in a poem we decide to call the firelight beautiful. No relationship at all. Nowadays, of course, the attempt *is* often made to make that relationship. The attempt is made to say that fire is beautiful *because* it burns. Or that love is beautiful *because* of the (spectrum of) sexual perversity. But I suspect that the curious way in which we can call anything beautiful – and by that means put Socrates and Plato into such a fix of having to justify the activity – points towards a supernatural explanation. It is as though we all live in the doom of a single, shared memory. Of course the supernatural and anamnesis feature in Socrates' and Plato's philosophy too: for it is difficult not to think of the World of the Forms as a supernatural place: and when they are pressed to explain the general human predilection for truth and why the philosophical impulse should rise to agitate any of us at all, they are led to conclude that the World of the Forms is somehow remembered by us, so that a large part of what any teacher does when teaching successfully is to reignite in his students its memory.[5]

However, I wish to continue to insist that what I mean by 'a single, shared memory' is different. I wish to insist that what we remember is not Beauty itself, in abstract, but some long lost experience of a time when our love would explode from our souls as a genuinely creative force. Francis Bacon once showed his exasperation against exactly this memory by writing:

And this is the manner of men, to pass over what lies before their feet, and look out for obscurities.[6]

Early Christian philosophers quickly learnt to talk about an *ordo amoris* – as though outside of us exists a concrete scheme of goodness, so that the corresponding responsibility on each of us is to work to give the ordinate affection back to each part of this scheme. At the same time you could find misfits like St. Augustine of Hippo, secretly appalled by this orthodoxy and inserting the contraflow to it whenever possible. The contraflow of what I have been calling the originality of a human life. Augustine, for example, was prone to write subversive things like this:

> Men go forth to marvel at the mountain heights; at huge waves in the sea they do the same. The same again at the broad expanse of flowing rivers, at the wide reaches of the ocean, and the circuits of the stars. Yet themselves they will pass entirely by.[7]
>
> For this heaven which we look up to with these eyes of ours, is not very precious before God. Holy souls are the heaven of God.[8]

By contrast, Socrates' and Plato's analogy of the cave flows in precisely the opposite direction. The beginning of its myth is the foetal position of the human race, huddled, helpless, helping itself. They want us to imagine a dark cave in which a group of men have been kept chained and innocent of anything else since earliest childhood. They face into the cave, looking onto a large wide wall; and they have been prevented from looking anywhere else all their lives by their restraints and also by strange devices like the blinkers we use on horses. Behind them stretches a long and narrow passage out into the open air and the light of day. But because of their unique conditions, they have never been aware of it. Behind them, also, is a curious apparatus for throwing shapes and sounds onto the wall they stare into. This consists of an elevated stage and walkway set back some distance from them. Between the walkway and their backs is a low parapet of a wall. Behind this wall, and up and down the walkway, process men, moving in slow crouches so that no part of their actual person will be seen above the wall. They do this so that only what they are holding will be seen above the wall. What they are holding are fabricated likenesses of things out in the 'real' world above the cave. These might be likenesses of inanimate objects like fruits. Or they might be statuettes of animals and even humans. Sometimes they add their own voices to the show – speaking human words or making other sounds. Why do they do all of this? They do it because set back behind their puppet show is a large fire, kept continuously burning. This fire illuminates the cave wall before the 'prisoners', huddling below it. And this fire also means that the puppet show appears before the men as moving shadows on that wall. The occasional voices and sounds also appear before the men as echoes responding from that wall. This wall and its effects, say Socrates and Plato, is the whole known world of these men. It is all they have ever known. Nothing has given them rise to question its status. And we notice then that in this, Socrates' and Plato's description of it, we are encountering the makings of a pitiful scene. And they have intended for this to be our reaction. For they know full well that we the readers have always lived outside the cave, which means that it is impossible for us not to encounter it now, in their analogy, from the fresh air of that advantage. Socrates and Plato know that we cannot but peer into that dankness and have a response of horror and anger. Who has allowed such a thing to happen to these men? Who is responsible (and his head on a plate!)? It is a brilliant and exciting analogy because it cuts us these clear, wide channels for our indignation to run into. And when indignation runs so effortlessly and unobstructed, there too, it is invariably assumed, will be found common sense and justice – common sense and justice in their purest forms.

Now the reason we can feel so indignant and clamour for justice under conditions like this analogy is something that I have already explained. It is because of the number system. We only have to ask: What crime is being committed here, in this analogy? The answer: The most heinous crime of all, the crime against modernization. These men are so clearly being kept in a state of innocence that it boils modernity's blood to see it. What it means to be human is to be able to be born into any imaginable situation and *still* impose on it the dreams and visions of tragedy, hope and redemption. Everyone knows this; it is why the human race has its history of songs and myths, religions and philosophies, science and the occupation of new planets. All of this happens because only humans take something from inside of their souls and choose to see through it into their actual, factual predicament in the world. Children, because they are most innocent (but not totally innocent), do this best of all. But it is not only the soul that works away inside the human animal: the mind works away as well. The mind contends with the soul to make the human project. Here, in the analogy of the cave by Socrates and Plato, we see the mind's victimizing of the soul – we see the mind's scorning of the foetal position of the human race.

What would not be preferable, say Socrates and Plato, than that one by one these men in the cave were to have their innocence taken away from them? Imagine just one of them, suddenly unchained, with his blinkers removed and turned around to face the light of the fire and all of the epiphany that that would bring on. This turning around of the first man is the turning point, also, of their whole analogy. It is intended to remind us of the unassailable truth that there is *always* a reality behind the reality which we at any moment inhabit. This is what the mind is peculiarly adapted to find out: and in the end its finding out is the only contribution that the mind is able to make. But you have to admit that there is an inescapable beauty in this business of moving through one reality to another, and its promise of going deeper and more truthful. And I hope that I am not making out by this that Socrates and Plato set out to manipulate us with their analogy and their philosophy. I hope it is clear that I am merely acknowledging how captivated they had become by this beauty of the music behind the music, the words behind the words – ever clearer, ever cleaner. Socrates and Plato could never have anticipated the ideology of the number system which takes over at this point: for the 'ideology of the number system' makes use of the sincere intentions of great thinkers like them. It suspends the parts of their conscience which might in another story have found surprising new sympathies with their prisoners – and with the foetal position in all its improvised self-sufficiency against Predestination.

Predestination tricks us by sweet words put into the mouths of good men. It insists that we must all be turned around to see the light. Once it really gets going, as by the means of the analogy of the cave, it goes so far as to say that it would be positively inhuman of any of us to insist to do otherwise. This, of course, is its greatest trick of all. But this is where it also makes its greatest mistake of all. For it underestimates the sheer damned glorious freedom we have to turn away from it, or to turn into it in hot wild fury and smash it in. Only a human being can will to do this mad crazy thing. Predestination, certain of everything else, is certain too that if we can just once be shown the light, and the meaning of good and evil, and all of that, then we will never want to go back to what we had before. But Predestination, for everything that it can see, cannot see freedom, cannot see joy, cannot see the extempore things that humans can initiate. It cannot even construct the idea that we would throw numbers, facts and truth back in its face like this. Predestination, because it sees everything, is blind to these moments that truly matter. It deals in truth, but humans deal in moments that truly matter: in possessiveness and love. Blood runs warm, but the glacial eye is icy and unmoved.

Socrates and Plato are led – by carefully calculated steps worked out in advance for them – into leaning mockingly on the processes and bonds that were originally designed to come about as a consequence of what I have called the 'projecting outwards of emotions from the human soul'. The confidence that Socrates and Plato have in their analogy at this point is to know that having depicted the men in the darkness as prisoners from the light, they can rely on our good-wishing to want them to be freed. This confidence allows them to indulge in some observations. They imagine the single prisoner who has been freed, and who has been turned around to face the fire and the whole bizarre mechanism of his abuse. They imagine him walking silently past his guards and torturers and down and up and out of the narrow passage into the open air – and the light of day. How the sun would strike him back at first and blind him! How he would run back terrified into the comfort and homeliness of the darksome depths! Oh the irony of it! In fact, knowledge of human nature tells us that to even get him up and out into the sunlight would require some good deal of force. But for the sake of the analogy, they say, let us imagine that force being applied. Let us imagine him dragged back up the narrow passage kicking and screaming and brought back out into the sun. Let us imagine him transfixed there until curiosity eventually got the better of him and he started to look about and compare this new reality to his experiences of old. This is where Socrates and Plato start to have some fun. They have him looking about him at the crisp and brilliant new look of things; and they have him shuddering to remember their pale shadow likenesses in the cave. No doubt the men in the cave had over time developed a method of distinguishing between themselves in relationship to this, their shadow-knowledge. Because this prideful way that humans have of wanting to elevate themselves is a given in any society. More than that: it *is* society: and most of what we call civilization describes the institutions into which we have allowed such meritocratic thinking to peacefully accrue –

Suppose there had been honours and citations that those below bestowed upon one another. Suppose prizes were offered for the one quickest to identify the shadows as they go by and best able to remember the sequence and configurations in which they appear. All these skills, in turn, would enhance the ability to guess what would come next. Do you think he would covet such rewards?[9]

You would have to say he would not, or at least, with some difficulty, some nostalgia and some tearing of heart. Certainly we can say what would soon happen to him were he actually to return to huddle with the citizens of his former civilization. We all know what happens when you go from streaming sunlight into the dark: you can hardly see for a time as your eyes make their adjustment. During this time of floundering and disability, would he not soon be laughed at and mistreated by his fellows for his 'weakened' perception? Would this not madden him like the grand injustice it would assuredly be? Wouldn't he want to curse his former family and friends, to denounce them as traitors to the truth, to inform on them and have them forcibly re-educated? I am using language stronger than Socrates and Plato ever used because I am building towards a point quite different from theirs. Injustice, or rather justice in its combination with the philosopher statesman's duty to truth, is famously the *Republic*'s leading concern, but the totalitarianism which results from it is a benign and well-meaning one; and the irritation about democracy from which that totalitarianism springs has been a valuable caveat for Western ideas. To provide some practical way for ontological moral knowledge to irradiate life – to combat mere sophistry and emptiness – was the mission objective for these men of genius. It was, and does continue to be, an important mission; and they were entitled to use every means at their disposal to accomplish it. But in and around their original mission have always existed the spaces for new missions, with valuable new objectives for new generations. Let me now in fact go directly to how they close their analogy of the cave, and then after that indicate what remains in and around it to do.

The cave and the life-changing experience of that single prisoner have illustrated the psychological and social effects of the call of philosophy. It is the thought that once thought cannot be got out of one's head. It reminds us that the first duty of the philosopher is to walk alone, immune and aloof to the dream-state and shadow-thinking of everyone else. For he has made his contact with the Form of the Good: and that must mean his total and immediate exemption from the normal architectures of perception in time, when first principles and the *a priori* are snatched up with religious zeal as truth, and lesser folk must squabble out their property rights over accidental knowledge, and all of it collided against them by the wheel of life anyway. But of course immunity and aloofness ridden out to their ends would create a monster out of the philosopher. And this is the point at which he realizes that he is going to have to have to remain a man of the cave after all – albeit the cave's educator and illuminator. This realization is the blow that keeps Plato's philosophy sane and practical. I have been talking of Socrates and Plato together thus far; but with this selfless choice that the true philosopher must be imagined to make each time (the choice to return to his city as its statesman rather than to disappear from it forever as its fugitive), we get to witness the strategic thinking of Socrates on ethics becoming very much the tactical thinking of Plato on politics. Socrates was the genius, the prophet, the muse, the virtuoso mind. He exemplified the extent to which the secret dream of all serious ethics is apartheid from all other minds; a state of citizenship with oneself; and the psychological flush of feeling right about everything. Some vague feeling of panic told Plato that what we mean by politics is much more to do with altruism and philanthropy. For on the one hand, we feel obliged to imagine that something as serious as politics must be argued, and won, to a hard-dry point of intellectual certainty. And notwithstanding that we may be able to convince ourselves of a certainty which includes toleration and other points of view as its subset – pluralism, say. But on the other hand, this convincing can never go far enough, because what we deep down really mean by a deadly serious thing such as politics and the optimal society is a warm wet earthy sort of feeling. The kind of blue and green you would see from space and realize was your home. If the virtue of intellection is that it is going to be like the rocket that will break us free from gravity and the ponderous, then what we have all along called happiness starts to look very much like the irony of the return journey back to earth. What other air could we breathe and still live?

Thus goes the crux of the analogy of the cave:

> Now, my dear Glaucon, we must apply the allegory as a whole to all that has been said so far. The prisoners' cave is the counterpart of our own visible order, and the light of the fire betokens the power of the sun. If you liken the ascent and exploration of things above to the soul's journey through the intelligible order, you will have understood my thinking, since that is what you wanted to hear. God only knows whether it is true. But, in any case, this is the way things appear to me: in the intelligible world the last thing to be seen – and then only dimly – is the idea of the good. Once seen, however, the conclusion becomes irresistible that it is the cause of all things right and good, and that in the visible world it gives birth to light and its sovereign source, that in the intelligible world it is itself sovereign and the author of truth and reason, and that the man who will act wisely in private and public life must have seen it.
>
> I agree, insofar as I can follow your thinking. [Glaucon]
>
> Come join me, then, in this further thought. Don't be surprised if those who have attained this high vision are unwilling to be involved in the affairs of men. Their souls will ever feel the pull from above and yearn to sojourn there ... [But remember] that the law is concerned not with the happiness of any particular class in the city but with the happiness of the city as a whole ... Because you have seen the reality of beauty, justice and goodness, you will be able to know idols and shadows for what they are. Together and wide awake, you and we will govern our city, far differently from most cities today whose inhabitants are ruled darkly as in a dream by men who will fight with each other over shadows and use faction in order to rule, as if that were some great good.[10]

The counter-intelligence of flesh and blood

What could you possibly say against all this resounding good sense except what I want to say against it: which is something that I want to put it in its place – a vital and continuing place, but a place nonetheless, for it must not have mastery over our souls. We look at this argument and see the Academy and the book of ethics that we will have the chance to author by our self-determination and personally put up high upon Academy's shelves. For without question that is the pull and the attraction in this kind of good sense. Once we were young and ancient and naive: and then we were old and modern and informed. And look, here is our book to prove it – the book of our examined life. And yet there have been some thinkers within the Western tradition who have tried to shatter this illusion for us. At the head of this chapter, I put the wisdom of one of them – Ludwig Wittgenstein – and something from his single glorious (he didn't write another) lecture on ethics. This idea that there is going to be a rainbow of books for us all to look back on one day, he says, is wrong. There are not going to be white books, and brown books, and black books, and yellow books; and even green books, and blue books, and red books. There is just going to be one book, because all this time, as well as all the conceivable time into the future, the only 'hand' that has been writing is Reason's hand. Invincible and uncaring and unsparing. And data by metadata it has been intent and hell-bent on turning our emotions into our *behaviours*; and then our behaviours into our *instincts*; and then, finally, our instincts into our indelible *genetics*. The Academy proclaims that ethics is something we can all aspire to: that it can be something that we make our own: that it can be like a kind of personal religion. But Wittgenstein says this is nonsense – for the whole point of God-less religion is to trick us. Like if you were to put down food every night in front of a wooden idol and instead the monkeys were to eat it. 'Ethics' was never meant to be a plural, or a collective, description; for at the point at which any ethic claims truth for itself it immediately becomes intolerant of even the faintest sniff of any rival to that claim. Any really brilliant attempt at ethics will bear this out and produce a dictatorship, which is of course what Plato's *Republic* shows truly enough in the end. By the same token, any true dictatorship ceases to be a human society at all for all its monism and becomes instead as still and soundless as a book. Wittgenstein's insight into this situation is to say that what we mean by ethics, virtue and perfection is really a supernatural aspiration: and that it turns disastrous on us once we insist on trying to find it in the natural empiricism of existence. The manifest certainty of the laws of the universe might encourage us to venerate them as objects of faith and hope (and the very picture of eternal reason), but Wittgenstein would believe that this is both impossible and unwise:

> It seems to me obvious that nothing we could ever think or say should be *the* thing. That we cannot write a scientific book, the subject matter of which could be intrinsically sublime and above all other subject matters. I can only describe my feeling by the metaphor, that, if a man could write a book on Ethics which really was a book on Ethics, this book would, with an explosion, destroy all the other books in the world. Our words used as we use them in science, are vessels capable only of containing and conveying meaning and sense, *natural* meaning and sense. Ethics, if it is anything, is SUPERNATURAL and our words will only express facts; as a teacup will only hold a teacup full of water and if I were to pour out a gallon over it.[11]

Didn't Charles Darwin put himself the opposite side of this insight in his *On the Origin of Species*? Didn't he put us all down on our knees in front of wooden idols offering food when he crossed that line (so easy to cross with words) and talked of Nature actually selecting things? Yes: just as though idols could eat, but far more beguiling in Darwin's case for all the ease with which it appeared to be able to overturn a paramount dogma of the Christian era. In Darwin's theory, the triumphant proof comes when the hand of Nature shows its unwavering superiority over the hand of Art. For Art is what the human soul throws out from its unreachable deeps. These deeps which cannot be understood are nonetheless seen in the coming together of human animals into their huddles – yes, even into the down-dark huddle of Socrates' and Plato's analogy of the cave. But against the Darwinian logic I have argued that these huddles are not ad hoc states of nature which we can brandish like the immemorial lesson of the modern age. They are each of them the outer projections of the inner truth that human behaviour is motivated by fantasy rather than anything else. This fantasy flourishes and is at its keenest in the ways in which children dream into life the ancient memory of this human race. All the distinctive things that the human animals do – their ability to form up a style of life even in the desperation of the damp and the dark with only shadows to go on – none of it is to be scoffed at. More than that, there is no logical way that it can be scoffed at: for as I have shown thus far, fantasy works in one direction and science works in the opposite direction. To say that 'Nature selects', even if only illustratively, is indeed like saying that the idols actually eat the food put down for them rather than the monkeys in the dead of night. Only humans can play the human game of willing and selecting – what I have called the game of possessiveness. Only humans can love in that way. Only humans can use their souls to overlay the natural world with the supernatural. Inanimate Nature cannot do this (so therefore there is nothing to be gained from admiring its 'efficiency' or 'intelligence'). And possibly this makes it that Sigmund Freud was right to consider that the subconscious activity of dream formation is the classic example of how the supernatural dominates and supervenes in the natural, and not Darwin's way round. For the defining feature of any dream is that naturally occurring events have been mixed together and overlaid with meaning. No one ever wakes up and thinks of a dream they had, that it was nonsense. Everyone secretly hopes to discover in it some meaning, some direction, to be read. In exactly the same spirit, not even Plato is allowed to present the prisoners in the cave as though they were merely a parody of the 'behaviours' (and yes the 'instincts' and the 'genetics') of association and belonging. What those prisoners were exhibiting in their feelings for one another came from some magical emotional source within them. And like the artists that all human beings are, they painted their astonishing and improbable significances into their apparently hopeless situation.

The truth is that we can't have it both ways. If those prisoners had actually painted pictures upon the walls of their cave, and we were studying them today, we wouldn't dare laugh at them – or point a moral about enlightenment at their expense. In the name of toleration and multiculturalism, we would probably be gushing about the esoteric qualities of their cave paintings. We would proclaim their art as a shadowy glimpse of the human psyche from across the ages; or something like that; though you know what I mean. Basically, my point is that you can't do all of that admiring and sympathizing whilst at the same time thinking with Darwin. Because for Darwin, human Art is swallowed up and pre-empted by Natural Selection. In just the same way that myth and religion are said to be swallowed up and pre-empted by final truth:

I have called this principle, by which each slight variation, if useful, is preserved, by the term Natural Selection, in order to mark its relation to man's power of selection. We have seen that man by selection can certainly produce great results, and can adapt organic beings to his own uses, through the accumulation of slight but useful variations, given to him by the hand of Nature. But Natural Selection...is a power incessantly ready for action, and is as immeasurably superior to man's feeble efforts, as the works of Nature are to those of Art.[12]

I can sum it all up by saying this: Western education conditions us to believe that the one meta-narrative – or the book that we are all scripted to write out for ourselves – is the story of how we will each of us break out from the prison according to our abilities. It does not take long to realize that every sane and self-evident success-path for us has been paved out in advance as a variation on this theme. It begins with growing up and leaving home. But am I the only one who thinks that the more naturally human meta-narrative would tell how we are really all trying to break back into a Prison? I don't think it matters what that Prison would be; or even if the fact of our wanting to break into it would transform its definition into that of 'Paradise' rather than 'Prison'. Please also don't confuse this with the patronizing way that Plato's philosopher statesmen return to their prison to do their job there. I am saying that the *Ur*-drama that really matters – the *Ur*-drama that allows us to collect and coordinate our thoughts about what it means to be human – is the story of the lengths that we will go to in order to break back into our spiritual Home. As I say, let's not try to imagine what that Home is and argue about it. But do let's please designate it as 'spiritual' – if only to signify that it doesn't need to care a damn about facts or the exigencies of life. I suspect that it would be quite prepared to make you take a bullet for it (a bullet for a dream), because against Natural Selection and the Number System and all such supercomputing certainty our bodies and our emotions are the only weapons that it has. I remember how the Russian writer Mikhail Bulgakov once came out with it in his fantastical short story *Diaboliad*. The hero of his story – Korotkov – fighting against an opposing hell of circumstances, each one predestinating him further and faster into his doom, comes to the wild conviction that speed unto death will be his winning contribution. Only the mind can make the body pause for thought: but the body (electric) can fling itself forward by some potent inner energy and intelligence of its own. It is all so brilliant of Bulgakov, because by this he somehow creates a character who leaps from the pages of the story into freedom. Even though Bulgakov has written a story that, like any story, you could turn to its end to learn its final truth, well, all of that possibility is vanquished in a flash by the counter-intelligence of flesh and blood that he puts into his character Korotkov:

> For about three seconds his head burned tormentingly, but then, remembering that no kind of sorcery should stop him, that stopping meant destruction, Korotkov moved towards the elevator.[13]

At this talk of final truth and its classic example in Darwin's principle of Natural Selection, I feel free to start folding the page of my story in half – exactly so that its edges line up perfectly on each other. The principle of Natural Selection is probably the most well-known emblem of the scientific dogma that all human ingenuity in the direction of make-believe, myth and emotion can be deconstructed from the point of view of some *Urstoff*. Some unblinking eye and blank identity against which human whimsy and personality formation can be seen as the greatest insult and THE capital crime.

After his invention and veneration, wasn't Socrates also put to death for being Socrates? Wasn't the very method of his invention also apparently the very method taken against him by his eventual accusers and enemies? Philosophy and the Good Life began in whimsy and personality, humanity and wonder. Once it had gotten properly under way and birthed classical Athens as the school of the world, it became a religion – more powerful than any that had come before it, and with real and increasing powers to instruct us in why we had to have it. I am quite prepared to go so deep into my metaphors as to say that Natural Selection killed Socrates once it had made enough use of him. It killed him with the same unblinking-blank purpose that it commits all of its crimes against human flesh and blood; and what I have called human flesh and blood's intrinsic counter-intelligence. Once Socrates began to exhibit in his spirit and personality the originality of a human life, his days were already numbered. In the Bible at Matthew 10.36 it is cryptically written: 'And a man's foes *shall be* they of his own household.' I have always taken this to be exactly what happened to Socrates.

Every act of sacrificial killing, one human to another, from Socrates to the Aztecs to the Nazi death camps, becomes shameful to us because we know it was committed within the single household of the brotherhood of man. The puzzle – and the fact that these killings will continue for as long as there are humans on earth – is the fact that the same logic that makes the concept of the single household possible (as the self-evidence of human rights) seems also to be the logic that overtakes our good heart towards each other when one of us – or a set of us – feels that we have come into the Way of Truth. At this moment, we really do seem to shed our personalities and take on the cold hard indifference of sharpened steel. Our consciences become absolved because we understand ourselves to be merely the occupants and functionaries of an office, so that the real hand on the sword becomes not ours but the very Hand of Truth. It becomes a strange, automatic way of being quite diametrically opposed to the real freedom within us, by which we know that we could at any moment turn around and stop the killing. We might of course be killed ourselves in the process. But it really is as simple as that. Didn't the Presocratic Heracleitus have something to say about this? Didn't he indicate that we have wars and killings in the first place because nothing has the capacity to prove us all into righteousness quite like them? To those who are killed, the event of it proves that they were right about its coming (and why). To those who kill, the stringency of the measure itself becomes the final proof of the finality of their cause. Inattention to this is perhaps one of the most serious shortcomings of modern-day historical explanation – its reason, too, for being unable to understand the standout cases of human evil en masse. It is not so much that the killings of the world wars become possible because killing is facilitated, by technology, into becoming impersonal. It is because in a world where everything can be made to appear relative, we find that we naturally reach, once our backs are against the wall or our blood is up, for a sacrament rather than an ethic. Death is a sacrament. And in the end, you can't fight your way out of anything with an ethic, but you can with a sword. The calm, peaceful, rational, butter-wouldn't-melt Good Life has been transported from age to age by civil wars and the sacrament of the sword; and don't we know the irony of it?

We are taught to believe that wars will one day be eradicated by ideas, or what is the same thing, by the diplomacy of ideas. But the deeper truth is that we only ever started having rational, ethical ideas when once it became possible to kill each other for them. Before Socrates was invented you had taboo, and its transgression, and killings that now look a lot like ritual if they don't look like murder. After Socrates was invented, this changed, and the world entered into this present age in which it has become a viable ambition to kill for ideas. Is it any surprise, for example, that what we today call 'rationality' takes all its sense and deportment from the threat of death? Or in its positive spin: Natural Selection? Let us please be brutally clear about this: It is only because the Way of Truth lets us into the self-knowledge that we would kill at the drop of a hat for the sovereignty and sway of our preferred version of the Way that we have the justification of what the philosophers call 'rational behaviour' in the first place. You can see it in the famous 'state of nature', or 'original position', arguments which explain submission and homologation (the two features of human society that really do need to be explained to anybody with the capacity to otherwise be an individual) in relation to our inborn 'fight or flight' instinct. Or you can see it in the more subtle arguments of, say, Jürgen Habermas, in which rationality is any form of inter-human communication where, instead of fighting to the death for your opinions and saying what you actually think, you plump for something dishonest that you can both accept.[14] I mentioned that the Presocratic Heraclitus had something to say about this, and as usual with the Presocratics, it cuts to the quick:

> War is the father of all and the king of all, and some he has made gods and some men, some bond and some free.[15]

Natural selection's *Urstoff*

Whenever it has come to singling out and classifying the first philosophers, historians of the subject from Aristotle on up have always looked for evidence of the kudos of *Urstoff* in a Darwinian style.[16] And with a man called Thales they have always found it. Thales is a good example, too, of how all that remains of these first philosophers are often snatches, or fragments, of their writings – preserved by good fortune in the later writings of others. In Thales' case, all his fragments have survived in this way. It is most reliably in Aristotle's *Metaphysics* that we learn that Thales believed the *Urstoff* to be water; and it is a little later in the same work that we find Aristotle's interesting little dig, a la Cornford, that you can find tantalizingly similar thoughts in far earlier, mythological material. That said, he seems content on further reflection to let this concern go, and to agree that what Thales was saying for water was a first; for it is one thing to say that water was in some important sense involved in the primeval processes of creation; but it is quite another thing to make the logical rather than the chronological statement that creation worked upon an always-existing 'God-particle', and that this was water.

> Yet these men [the pre-Socratics] do not all give the same account either of the number of such primordial beings or of what kind of being they have. Thales, the pioneer in this kind of philosophy, declares that the primordial being is water (and therefore proclaimed the earth to be on water), probably having this idea suggested to him by the fact that the nutriment of everything is moist and that heat itself is born out of the moist and is kept alive by it.[17]
>
> Some think that those ancients who, long before the present generation, were the first to theologize, had a similar idea of nature; because they presented Ocean and Tethys as the parents of becoming and water as that by which the gods swore, which these people styled the 'Styx.' For what is oldest is most honourable, and what anyone swears by is the most honourable. [However] although it may not be clear whether this opinion about nature is primitive and ancient, Thales at any rate is said thus to have explained the principles and origins of things.[18]

Another, more succinct description of Thales' innovation, this time preserved by Seneca:

> For he [Thales] said that the world is held up by water and rides like a ship, and when it is said to 'quake' it is actually rocking because of the water's movement.[19]

I recorded in the last chapter that Thales was born in Miletus sometime in the seventh century B.C. – in the region of ancient

Greece called Ionia, or what is today Izmir Province in Turkey. In fact all we know of Thales in terms of dates is that he was in his acme at around 585 B.C., when he is recorded to have correctly predicted an eclipse of the sun using his skills in astronomy and geometry; and also, presumably, by having access to a decent backlog of astronomical data. This data could have been acquired from the written records of Babylonian priests, perhaps during a visit to Sardis. Or also from Egyptian priests. For of course the geographical position of Miletus was significant because it gave it an overland connection to Sardis and what that city represented as a cultural gateway to Asia and the East. Egypt could be reached by sea; and indeed Miletus had excellent trading links with the port settlement at Naucratis – a Greek trading colony on the Nile Delta permitted by the Egyptians since at least the seventh century B.C. This colony was located about 70 km from the Mediterranean coastline, and seems to have been to the Greeks a little like what Hong Kong was to the British in relation to China. Interestingly, it would remain something of an 'open' colony throughout its history. No one Greek city-state owned it in league. And from Herodotus comes the information that at least 12 Greek city-states had their representatives and rights there – all of them city-states from the Eastern Mediterranean like Miletus.[20]

Socrates, of course, was born c. 469 B.C., dying in 399 B.C. I don't want to sound too facetious here, but by making his acme around the age of 30, and subtracting that date from Thales' acme, you could say that it took roughly 150 years to invent Socrates.

Thales predicted eclipses and went down in his own lifetime as legendary in practical ingenuity and traditional wisdom. He took on commissions and gave out advice. Herodotus has written up two examples of this. In the one, Thales advises the Ionians to keep to a single deliberative chamber at Teos; and to which all the other Ionian cities of the League can be related as demes.[21] In the other (which Herodotus did not in fact believe), he is credited with helping Croesus' army ford the river Halys. Thales was said to have been in the army at the time. He realized that the river which faced the army could be made fordable if part of its flow was diverted around and behind them by means of a bypassing channel. This channel was duly dug and sure enough: the river halved its flow and the army crossed to the other side.[22]

It is important to separate out two general points from this information. Babylonia and Egypt had the reputation with the classical Greeks as special places of intellectual sophistication. The Babylonians were brilliant astronomers and the Egyptians were just as brilliant geometers and land-measurers. They controlled the Nile and had built the pyramids. In the case of pioneer savants like Thales, it was de rigueur to have made some beginning with one of these traditions; preferably to have travelled there and been dipped into them firsthand. Either this actually happened; or, as was often the case, it was simply assumed that it must have happened by later ancient authorities. Second, and related to this, is the truth of what the first philosophers were innovating on. When the birth of Western philosophy is talked of as a giant moment in history; and especially when its giant stature is made by contrasting it with the 'religion and myth' that went before; it can be forgotten that Europeans before Thales were not primitives. It can be forgotten that there was no before and after measured in a widespread epiphany, or a clear dividing.

All this book long I have been hammering away at this with my anxiety that ancient and modern don't need to exist; save as some cunning way for us to inflict our superiority on the past and settle a score with the Unknown God.[23] Now I am going to get to 'fold the pages of my story in half', as I put it a little earlier, and start imagining what doors we closed on ourselves when we designated an historical moment for the birth of philosophy, for the number system, natural selection and the end of make-believe. Because as I have tried to explain thus far – and most particularly, here, in relation to the sacramental status of the 'analogy of the cave' in Western education – this new power to see backwards and forwards of our present position in terms of relations of cause and effect (and the reams of facts that must feed this machine) cannot be exercised at the same time as the other, supernatural powers of the human being, which I have consistently described under the term 'soul'. In fact, I go so far as to say that the new power has a cunning and intelligence of its own: and that it expresses both these attributes as it shows how it is hell-bent on destroying us. This destruction, when it is finally visited, will be seen in how we have become everything but the 'body electric'. It will no longer be that 'history' is the concept whose very uniformities and laws inflame us to disregard it, the better to regard with keener intensity ourselves in each other. No: instead of that magic which can marshal all our resources of love and dreaming, we will have been rendered useful only to give to history the machine's 'habitual reaction' – to use a phrase from A. E. Taylor.[24] We won't have been left with nothing, of course; for we will have the machine's invincibility of purpose; where that same purpose will become the very 'rationality' with which we are able to mock to scorn and besiege the last few lovers, and the last few dreamers. They will point to each other as proof of what they hope in. We will point to numbers and negate ourselves. Just look at what happened when the Marxist intellectual George Plekhanov wrote his powerful essay *The Role of the Individual in History*. Just look at how he points at numbers to deliver his coup de grace:

> Until the individual has won *this* freedom by heroic effort in philosophical thinking he does not fully belong to himself, and his mental tortures are the shameful tribute he pays to external necessity that stands opposed to him. But as soon as this individual throws of the yoke of this painful and shameful restriction he is born for a new, full and hitherto never experienced life; and his *free* actions become the *conscious and free expression* of necessity...Again, being conscious of the absolute inevitability of a given phenomenon can only increase the energy of a man who sympathizes with it and who regards himself as one of the forces which called it into being. If such a man, conscious of the inevitability of this phenomenon, folded his arms and did nothing, he would show that he was ignorant of arithmetic.[25]

Beginning with Thales, the Presocratics' story has been presented to Western audiences as Reason's triumphant foundation myth; the changing of the guard; and a brave new world for ever after. But the truth is that it is much less of a mechanical, and therefore much more of a human, story than that. Thales can be the start, yes. But the start of something that reads a lot more like a fairy tale, pointing a moral. Like all fairy tales, this one is made possible because the human component in it doesn't change one bit. Which may come as a surprise, when the point of its traditional telling was to reinforce the opposite idea: that its main characters – Thales et al. – were the representatives of a humanity waking up one day and determined to act as though fairy tales should be left behind forever, in childhood. But I am prepared to hang everything on the counterpunch that deep down *we just know* that the essence of humanity is not its ability to evolve itself in the direction of the better and the best, but the 'mirror effect' of the body electric. We are not fantastic because we are the ape who stopped scratching himself, and worked it all out, and ended up as we are now. We are fantastic because deep down *we just know* what the human touch looks and feels like. We can pick up a piece of knapped flint on a beach from goodness knows how long ago, and weigh its shape in our hand, and recognize that it was done by one of us, and how. In no logical way can this be a statement against the modern theory of evolution, by the way. My statement orbits within a different universe altogether. I am not offering with it the definitive guide to working out when (and if) the ape world slipped into the human. I am capturing the truism that you would be able to see yourself in the first human, but not in the last ape, which means, in turn, that the essence of humanity is this fact rather than all that we invest in principles that purport to be able to allow us to measure a single distance across both, like Natural Selection.[26] And this, finally, is what inspires me to read the Presocratics in a fairy-tale way. In other words, in a way unencumbered by the requirement to plot out some track of human advancement, but rather, in a way that secures that they were humans doing what humans do precisely because they were able to fall into this thing called philosophy and get themselves into all sorts of bother by it – new clarities, but also new, existential confusions. Just as humans would. Like in a fairy tale, theirs was a moral falling, or turning. They happened to take one fork in a road. They did not take that road because they were radio-controlled to by some world mind outside of them, or some evolutionary principle inside them, but because they freely chose to. Maybe when I finish writing this book I will turn my back on philosophy forever and go back into the cave. I could do that: you could do that: anyone could do that. We are not predestinated – though the Western way of writing about ideas has conditioned us to think as though we were!

As long as there are humans, there will be the stories of how humans fell into and out of things like philosophy. And from each of these stories, it will afterwards be possible to draw some lesson and wisdom – and in each case, the possibility to draw the lesson and wisdom will show that the human story that we can most naturally and satisfyingly follow is the one in which we have great adventures of the mind and spirit but stay essentially the same. Stand still and look as far backwards and as far forwards in time as you can. Now tell me what you see. You tell me that you see people just like you. That's because people just like you *are* the increments of your seeing; or to put it in the argument of this chapter, you see creatively, in a way that beams from the inside of you outwards. One of the most widely known set of Presocratic fragments outside the professional Academy comes from Xenophanes, and they say just this. Let me give them here:

> Homer and Hesiod have attributed to the gods all things that are a shame and a disgrace among mortals, stealings and adulteries and deceivings of one another.[27]
>
> But mortals deem that the gods are begotten as they are, and have clothes like theirs, and voice and form.[28]
>
> The Ethiopians make their gods black and snub-nosed; the Thracians say theirs have blue eyes and red hair.[29]
>
> Yes, and if oxen and horses or lions had hands, and could paint with their hands, and produce works of art as men can do, horses would paint the forms of the gods like horses, and oxen like oxen, and make their bodies in the image of their several kinds.[30]
>
> One God, the greatest among gods and men, neither in form like unto mortals nor in thought.[31]
>
> Always He remains in the same place, moving not at all; nor is it fitting for Him to go to different places at different times, but without toil He shakes all things by the thought of His mind.[32]

Or you could use Parmenides' rendition of the 'parallel worlds theory' as the illustration:

> (We must suppose that) men have been formed and the other animals that have life; and that the men have inhabited cities and cultivated fields, just as we have here; and sun and moon and so on, just as we have; and that the earth brings forth for them all manner of produce, of which they garner the best into their houses and use it. So much, then, have I said here about the process of

separating off – that separation would have taken place not only here with us but elsewhere too.[33]

The increments of your seeing are not, and cannot be, the facts of what is physically going on in the world around you. Nor can your religion and faith and good life be the extent to which you can bring yourself into correspondence, and dependence, upon those facts. If you could see it all in that way, you would see straight to the cancer lying in wait for you or the bullet with your name on it. This knowledge would destroy you. There would be no more 'Dear Diary...', as I put it at the close of the last chapter. No more of the beauty of not-knowing: no more 'Does she love me?' No more 'Is she like this with all men?' If you don't believe me, reread a thinker like Bertrand Russell. Ask yourself whether all his ecumenism isn't just *The Last White Man*? Because to me, what it seems to be offering to all of us is the chance to be so dispassionate, so aloof and then again so aristocratic that we should be proud (at the end of it all) to be wearing the one-size-fits-all mask of a white, male face. And when once you have considered this, ask yourself whether Russell's philosophy of life and morals doesn't now read something like this *Last White Man's* shrill extinction song? For all his talk of scientific good sense, for all his educationist zeal, when Russell really hits his fluency, it is arguably this fluency of the great high priest standing over naive realism – naive realism conceived as childhood's shocking sacrifice. What Russell calls 'creative idealism' is meant to be the knife to its heart and the superior truth standing over it. And it is his willingness to mock childhood and its innocence that makes Russell's personal ministry of the Religion of the Good Life such a case in point. And as with Socrates and Plato earlier in the chapter, I do not mean this to be an attack on Russell's sincere good intentions, or for that matter, his philosophical brilliance. I intend it to be a noteworthy example of how the sincere good intentions of only the very best of thinkers are for that very same reason the most vulnerable of all to be commandeered by a certain logic – or even something more sublime – until they are made to speak a language not their own. Yes, even the most ardent rationalist among them will find that he has developed a worship after all. And it is this irony that I want to draw attention to now, and nothing else.

Incidentally, the only protection against this, I imagine, would be for philosophy to try not to be so serious as to 'empty the haunted air' – as the poet Keats put it. Non-fiction should leave deadly seriousness well alone. The value of literature and fiction (and the esoteric fragments of long gone poet-philosophers) is that they can be our escape from realism. While the same holds vice versa. And we need escapes in both directions. A happy childhood will live on in memory as the useful example that the former direction of escape really did happen once; and can therefore happen again. We need to be able to believe in ghosts and miracles: and soldiers do cry for their mothers on the battle field. Make-believe will not become better by striving to be more realistic: it will simply cease to be make-believe at all. Someone who saw from the off that this mutual exclusivity and division of labour could bring us into new speeds and efficiencies of action was Niccolò Machiavelli.[34] But I want to end here with Russell's worship, as it will leave me in the place where I want to begin the next chapter.

> To every man comes, sooner or later, the great renunciation. For the young, there is nothing unattainable; a good thing desired with the whole force of a passionate will, and yet impossible, is to them not credible. Yet by death, by illness, by poverty, or by the voice of duty, we must learn, each one of us, that the world was not made for us, and that, however beautiful may be the things we crave, Fate may nevertheless forbid them. It is the part of courage, when misfortune comes, to bear without repining the ruin of our hopes, to turn away our thoughts from vain regrets. This degree of submission to power is not only just and right: it is the very gate of wisdom... And such thought makes us free men; we no longer bow before the inevitable in Oriental subjection, but we absorb and make it a part of ourselves. To abandon the struggle for private happiness, to expel all eagerness of temporary desire, to burn with passion for eternal things – this is emancipation, and this is the free man's worship. And this liberation is effected by contemplation of Fate; for Fate itself is subdued by the mind which leaves nothing to be purged by the purifying fire of time.[35]

3

The Soul of Blood

O soul come back to watch the birds in flight!
He who has found such manifold delights
Shall feel his cheeks aglow
And the blood-spirit dancing through his limbs.

'THE GREAT SUMMONS', *CHINESE POEM OF THE 2ND OR 3RD CENTURY B.C.*, ANON. (TRANS. ARTHUR WALEY)

How would you write the story of the first philosophers without the feeding frenzy that I have been describing – right up the food chain to the very top and *The Last White Man*? I suggest that you would have to mix the soul with blood. Or what is more, recognize that the human soul is already mixed with blood; that it is even in some back-to-front way *of* blood. I think if you can do this, if you can bring the flesh back into the story then you can end religion's hold over its telling – A Free Man's Worship, and all the rest. I think this is the way to go. No more miracles, no more discoveries, no more mind over matter. And especially no more doctrines and peripeties and schools of thought. I am tempted to say: 'Just what really happened.' But that is not quite what I mean, and nothing is ever like that. Perhaps I can draw out a better sense of purpose by making a dynamic comparison between my approach and that of Giambattista Vico in his remarkable *The New Science*.[1]

Giambattista Vico and piety

The New Science, first published in 1725, went rather underappreciated in Vico's time, though it gave considerable provocation. This is not the case today, when it can be roundly praised as a legitimate and discernible forerunner of the kind of materialist and societal view of human development that Marx was to perfect. There is a propaedeutic opening called 'Idea of the Work', in which Vico introduces what is to come with reference to a frontispiece. This gives a visual depiction of his New Science as well as clearly showing what is to be innovative or unsettling in the coordination of its four principal elements. At the top left of the illustration is the unblinking eye of God, which is taken to mean also divine providence and revelation. From it, beaming diagonally down and right is an illuminating ray. This ray strikes a convex jewel, hung about the breast of a striking lady called Metaphysic. She has winged temples and is standing atop a globe, which represents the physical world of nature and human institutions from family on up. From her jewel, the illuminating ray is reflected and refracted down and left. A substantial part of it hits a statue of the Greek poet Homer. Other more refracted parts spread out across various hieroglyphic representations of some obvious and pregnant symbols of human experience: an altar; fire and water; a *lituus* – which is the Latin name for the traditional augurs' staff; a lit torch to stand for marriage; a cinerary urn to stand for burial; a plough; a rudder to stand for the migrations of peoples; a tablet with inscribed letters to stand for literature; and then at the bottom of the scene and thus, as it were, the nearest to our own times, some hieroglyphs for 'modern' gentile civilization (where by 'gentile', he means all nations from the time of the non-Hebraic descendents of Noah onwards). These are a Roman fasces, a purse, a sword, a balance and a herald's caduceus. The last is probably the only one that needs an immediate word of explanation. For it, Vico had in mind a pre-civilized situation, prior to the establishment of settled governments, whether monarchical or popular, in which the primal law of might saw different peoples going at each other like pirates. A time, then, before the regulation of war and its declaration by advance party: a time before delegations, and leagues and treaties of peace. And therefore a time before the herald and his caduceus. In using it as a hieroglyph for modern gentile civilization, he therefore meant it to stand for the opposite of those pre-civilizational things: namely, for diplomacy, commerce and the balance of powers. Considered altogether, these hieroglyphs give Vico's ambition away for a science whose *Urstoff* and (universal) sweep will be found in the truth that human beings are code-bearing creatures. In other words, human traits have not been passed on like a baton relay, through physical proximity and dissemination by example. What Vico calls the 'world of nations' becomes proof instead for that world being in a sense ontologically prior to the advent of man. The axiom of his New Science is that you may scatter human beings like seed to all corners and environments of the earth, but what will spring up in every case are nations that are invariably reducible to hieroglyphic, or symbolic, representation. Didn't the symbolist Charles Baudelaire write that

> Nature's a fane where down each corridor/of living pillars, darkling whispers roll,/– a symbol forest every pilgrim soul/must pierce, 'neath gazing eyes it knew before.[2]

This clearly was the same kind of intrigue that Vico's mind was instinctively going after a century before. A story of the human condition made out of a handful of solemn, gigantic pieces; and a science of it based on the certainty that those pieces have retained their essential integrity through age after age. As for these ages, Vico's imagination for this sort of thing naturally inclined him to take as revelatory fact the ancient Egyptian wisdom that three distinct ages had given rise to this present one in which we now all find ourselves. These ages were: (1) 'the age of the gods'; (2) 'the age of the heroes'; and (3) 'the age of men'.[3] He at once took this triad as the template which you can lay over any accumulated human history to show you what has really been happening. Gods and heroes and men may be given different names in different parts of the planet, but this is merely cosmetic; and a trained application of the triad will demonstrate that behind every variety of human behaviour and self-expression is the codebook – *The New Science*:

> There will then be unfolded before us, not the particular history in time of the laws and deeds of the Romans or the Greeks, but (by virtue of the intelligible *substance* in the diversity of their

modes of development) the ideal history of the eternal laws which are instanced by the deeds of all nations in their rise, progress, maturity, decadence, and dissolution [and which would be so instanced] even if (as is certainly not the case) there were infinite worlds being born from time to time throughout eternity. Hence we could not refrain from giving this work the invidious title of a *New Science*, for it was too much to defraud it unjustly of the rightful claim it had over an argument so universal as that concerning the common nature of nations...[4]

All such totalizing sciences of the human condition begin in an itch, or an irritation – and Vico's was to be no different. In his case, the itch was his immense frustration that the truth of human affairs had somehow become unhitched from the *experiencing* of it. Let me explain this general case that Vico believed he was retaliating against. We must begin by acknowledging that because one of the chief requirements of the developed human mind is to keep us in the flow of a continuous sensation of our past, present and future (so that we can learn, be and plan ahead), it can for that very reason start to lead us to place its contents in a timeless and eternal frame of reference. That is to say, axioms, principles and theories can start to take on the characteristics of things prior and independent of us, so that finally they appear actually to have been blowing in to us from some divine place never changing, on some divine wind always with us. If, for example, I mention Cartesian rationalism, and furthermore, if I remember that Descartes' own illustration of his philosophical science was essentially the upside-down picture of Vico's frontispiece, then the nature of Vico's ambition against his age becomes clear. In the Prefatory Letter to his *Principles of Philosophy*, Descartes reinforces what he had always implied in his method: that things like the practical experience of civilization come last, and can only be established to be enjoyed on the rational first principles that inform them, and that are their sure foundations. Therefore,

> Philosophy as a whole is like a tree; of which the roots are Metaphysics, the trunk is Physics, and the branches emerging from this trunk are all the other branches of knowledge. These branches can be reduced to three principal ones, namely, Medicine, Mechanics, and Ethics (by which I mean the highest and most

perfect Ethics, which presupposes a complete knowledge of the other branches of knowledge and is the final stage of Wisdom). Now, just as it is not from the roots or from the trunk of trees that one gathers fruit, but only from the extremities of their branches, so the principal usefulness of Philosophy depends upon those parts of it which can only be learned last.[5]

Vico sets out to do the opposite. In his *New Science*, he sets out to begin from those parts of philosophy 'which can only be learned last'. And make no mistake that he is itched and irritated. In his frontispiece, 'Metaphysic' is really only as much as how God sees through our mutable minds the extent of what He has created good in the world. In turn, the eyes of our minds are really only as much as how we discern in the course of human history the acting out of a preordained series of developments. This is why the ray beams from God's eye to the convex jewel on the lady Metaphysic's breast. Then why again it beams from there in reflected and refracted ways onto all the various parts of constructed human behaviour down the ages. But Vico's system is a New Science: so what does this mean for the contents of its knowledge? Well, it means that knowledge will learn to respect, even to embrace, its paradoxical nature. This is where Vico positions the maverick insight that will inform his whole project. All scientific knowledge is a paradox because it purports to assemble in our minds a perfect rendition of the real. But this is blasphemy following upon nonsense, because only God's unblinking eye can have that vision. We may think that we attain to it in mathematics, but mathematics and logic are like stories that we make up by using symbols for words. These stories may truly enough reveal the consistency, or the rationality, of the real in action, but this makes them also just proverbial and instructive, like Lewis Carroll's *Alice's Adventures in Wonderland*. By the same token, physics, because it is inductive, could never conceive nor run the super-experiment that would prove everything once and for all – though the Hadron Collider will try. For that very super-experiment, says Vico, was God's prerogative in creating the world! What then can the human mind hope for when it seeks after truth? It can hope, Vico thinks, to discover its certainties in the one world that the human hand can rightfully claim to have crafted. This is what he calls the world of civilization and all its contrivances. Notice the historicist assumption that underpins this and gives Vico's New

Science its peculiar flair. Vico doesn't mean that in crafting their world of civilization, men did something independently of God. He means that God acted through them to do it; and that this process has left behind it a history and a set of spoor that we can track through the archaeology of human thinking. This archaeology is what is represented in his frontispiece illustration by the statue of Homer and the hieroglyphs. His itch and his irritation has been that the rationalist science of Descartes and the seventeenth century was not prepared to get its hands dirty in this material. It was too beguiled by the idea that the properly trained human mind could shoot clean through to the main prize and the first principles of things. When all along the real beginning, he was sure, would be to realize that

> The great fragments of antiquity, hitherto useless to science because they lay begrimed, broken, and scattered, shed great light when cleaned, pieced together, and restored.[6]

From 1699 until his death, Vico held the Chair in Rhetoric at the University of Naples. He was an expert philologist, so for him these 'great fragments of antiquity' – the set of 'spoor' – were the idea-patterns of the classical and pre-classical mind, and their subsequent dressing in language. This secured the importance to him of Homer, and what Homer could represent of the birth of Western literature. But as I have said, there was something genuinely Marxian and historicist about Vico's outlook. The seventeenth century had been the age of reason, from Galileo to Leibniz; and in terms of philosophy and human science that had meant the putting into practice of strictly quantitative and abstract methods of enquiry. The scholasticism which it superseded had been more qualitative, that is more deferential to the sentimental concept of 'timeless wisdom' – the idea that the ancients were closer than us to the source of all things, so that they breathed an altogether purer air, which we might savour ourselves by respecting their proximity to the gods. Vico didn't think this; but at the same time he also couldn't go along with the seventeenth-century philosophers' confidence in universal reason. For example, he couldn't go along with natural law theorists like Hugo Grotius, John Selden and Samuel von Pufendorf, whom he would explicitly chide for having eternalized law itself; as though the lights of conscience had been there all along in the minds of the earliest humans – just waiting to be switched on.[7] Nor could he accept what Hobbes set out to achieve of a 'civil philosophy' in his *De cive* of 1642. Hobbes depicted the state of nature as a wilderness of philosopher-men: as though they were already fitted out with the mental means of contract-making and delegation, and had only to stop and engage the cool hard thoughts of their rational best interests. The problem, for Vico, with both these examples of pure rationality was that they chose to ignore a crucial fact – for him, *the* crucial fact. This was that the human animal never was a numbers machine. Those great fragments of antiquity – exemplified in Homer – showed an altogether different view of the native intelligence of the species. They showed that the aboriginal spirit of man was mystical, was poetical. These people were not stupid relative to our modern-day clever, thought Vico; the truth was that they were actually creative relative to our modern-day reductive:

> The most sublime labour of poetry is to give sense and passion to insensate things; and it is characteristic of children to take inanimate things in their hands and talk to them in play as if they were living persons. This philologico-philosophical axiom proves to us that in the world's childhood men were by nature sublime poets.[8]

More than that: it was of the essence of Vico's plan to show that this creativity is dynamically involved in God's supernatural piloting of human affairs. If reason really was everything that the seventeenth century and its philosophers made it out to be – all penetrating and all seeing – then it might come one day to override God and prove that we can guide ourselves securely on our own instruments. This thought upset Vico; though not, we must note, because of conventional piety, but because it seemed to him to be so obviously, so mechanically, wrong. He knew that he was living in the great age of modernity, with all that it had gleaned about the world, and with the heightened opportunities for realism that this could bring ('What it requires of us is that, from these human times of acute and intelligent minds in which we are born, we should here at the end look back to the picture that was placed at the beginning.'[9]). But he had a strange and powerful instinct for bringing his New Science back always to the place that I designated a little earlier as the 'unhitching' of the truth of things from the experiencing of them. Pure rationalism creates a timeless man in the image of an Eternal Reason: yet Vico wanted to find a beginning, plus a way of pegging aboriginal man to that beginning: and then over and above that, a way to re-establish God in the role of the cunning manipulator. How he was to do this in the end must surely stand as one of the most original contributions to the question of the conscious and unconscious states of being – and therefore also to the question of which came first. Vico is emphatic: God came first. Then only after God came the phenomenon within which we have all been permanently fixed ever since – the phenomenon called human consciousness and time. Had Adam and Eve not sinned, things might have gone differently. But they did; and that has left it that the human animal remains in the natural state of having its back turned to God, believing its parts and consciousness to describe the extent of all understanding and knowledge. Every human being is born into the urgency of needing to create their own world from the ground up; or failing that, and when knowledge must be sought from others, to devising criteria for verifying as believable what these others say or write. This, indeed, is freedom to us now. This is what the experience of freedom feels like. It feels like choosing to love someone, to start a family with them, to found a city, to frame laws and so on and so forth. It means doing all these things for real, in the sense that God is nowhere to be seen. The atheists and agnostics are right to make capital out of this. But for Vico it is all just a wheel within a wheel, and God's wheel motivating ours, and not the other way round. Consider this, prosecuted by Vico on the entire hieroglyphic – that is the entire linguistic – history of the inner wheel, our world:

> It is noteworthy that in all languages the greater part of the expressions relating to inanimate things are formed by metaphor from the human body and its parts and from the human senses and passions... The farmers of Latium used to say the fields were thirsty, bore fruit, were swollen with grain; and our rustics speak of plants making love, vines growing mad, resinous trees weeping. Innumerable other examples could be collected from all languages. All of which is a consequence of our axiom that man in his ignorance makes himself the rule of the universe, for in the examples cited he has made of himself an entire world.

So that, as rational metaphysics teaches that man becomes all things by understanding them (*homo intelligendo fit omnia*), this imaginative metaphysics shows that man becomes all things by *not* understanding them (*homo non intelligendo fit omnia*); and perhaps the latter proposition is truer than the former, for when man understands he extends his mind and takes in the things, but when he does not understand he makes the things out of himself and becomes them by transforming himself into them.[10]

The dynamic of the 'wheel within the wheel', as I am describing it, says that at no point in human history is it ever possible for one single mind to reach up into the heavens and apprehend all things at once, and rationally, like a set of master plans spread out upon a table. Even if modern man may aspire to such a vision, and even if nearly 300 years on from Vico he has produced plans for most things, he is not in actual fact seeing beyond the wheel of time. As per the frontispiece in *The New Science*, God may on His whim illuminate our understanding by seeing through us to what he has made. And *The New Science* as a system of knowledge has presumably benefitted from this. But fundamentally His wheel turns our wheel by making use of the fact (I called it the crucial fact earlier) that fallen, and sinful, and proud, we are *creatively* intentioned. God makes use of this by allowing us to think that we are in full control of creating one thing when ultimately we are just furnishing the staging post to some other. Every sensation that tells us that we are the masters of our own destinies is a true sensation: and here is where the constructivists of today applaud Vico, and rightly so. But it is out of the very belligerence of his constructivism, out of his very diatribe against Cartesian natural philosophy and all its imitators and heirs, that Vico finds the wheel within the wheel. He says that you only have to begin where the matter really does begin, which for the postlapsarian human animal is the self-conscious experience of life. For all the other animals, the world as it is can be a natural home, in which they may play their unthinking parts. But man can have no natural home in this world of seasons, and predators and volcanoes. Left alone and naked, he would be wiped out by things he cannot automatically understand. With all the fauna and flora he shares the instinct to survive; but in his case, that instinct is all that he shares in. Science still has no access to the automatism even of the fragile monarch butterfly, which accomplishes a staggering migration from Canada to Mexico, in an imperious feat of strength and navigation. Consequently, man's history as a species begins as he applies himself to *create* a world in which he can hold down a natural home. This is the world of mud turned into bricks, and bricks turned into cities. Vico's seminal point is that the beauty and majesty of creations such as butterflies are of God: and therefore that you should not – indeed you cannot – deign to understand them. What you can deign to understand and still be pious and God-fearing is the constructed world of nations.

This shows what I earlier called the 'peculiar flair' of Vico's vision. Indeed we normally associate such thoroughbred constructivism as his with the elegant desperation of the historical visions of the 1930s and 1940s. In them the age of liberty has somehow twisted itself into the age of ideology. History is now appreciably manmade and Godless, but not yet triumphant in the way that it will start to be in the post Second World War recovery, when the staggering technologies of that war such as penicillin and computing, mass production and rocketry will develop into our speeds and securities of twenty-first-century living. Before getting back to Vico, let me just then quote this from H. A. L. Fisher's 1936 *A History of Europe*:

> Men wiser and more learned than I have discerned in history a plot, a rhythm, a predetermined pattern. These harmonies are concealed from me. I can only see one emergency following upon another as wave follows upon wave, only one great fact with respect to which, since it is unique, there can be no generalizations, only one safe rule for the historian: that he should recognize in the development of human destinies the play of the contingent and the unforeseen... The fact of progress is written plain and large on the page of history; but progress is not a law of nature. The ground gained by one generation may be lost by the next. The thoughts of men may flow into the channels which lead to disaster and barbarism.[11]

Compare this now to Vico's algorithm for calculating the principles of his New Science. He has noticed that as the Western mind develops into its secular maturity, it consistently begins to measure its efforts by its sophistication in differentiating between fiction and non-fiction. He has noticed, too, that the primal motivation of this is original sin itself. All the advantages of having fictional and non-fictional outlets are advantages *in medias res*. For non-fiction plots to one day hold an account of all possible reality; but only to leave it that fiction can be a little box with just God left inside it. Those last two thoughts on the theme of international conspiracy are my own. Vico's piety takes the form of saying that secularism's customary practice of categorizing fiction as imaginative, but non-fiction as empirical, is misleading. God has allowed man both the authorship and copyright in the roof over his head (and the whole world of such devices), because that is the very same mechanism that will keep man in perpetual dark about the final things of God, or the outer wheel's turning. If man was not thus free to create, free to be as atheist and agnostic as he likes, his knowledge would have to take the form of God's. This is precisely the road that Vico thinks pure rationalism sets out on, however God-fearing its intentions are. In light of this, the ultimate, correctional aspect of Vico's New Science becomes its argument that the further non-fiction gets projected beyond roofs over heads and the world of nations, the weaker and more fantastic it becomes. The reason this happens is because non-fiction is at bottom just fiction. A mud brick you can bake is the same as a story you can make up. It is just that mud bricks went on to become the world we actually inhabit, and the building blocks of its rules. A story can't protect you from the wind; and neither can you eat it. But that turns out to be the only difference that matters. The present consensus that there is no God; and that there is no God because non-fiction's territory now takes in everything that we call reality, so that He and fantasy in general have been squeezed out (except for children's amusement, or adults wanting to be like children and the financial gain to be had thereof); well, this present consensus never imagines that its *hypotheses* and *conjectures* might be of exactly the same order as that which it so proudly squeezes out. All of which doesn't disbar its activities (inductive or deductive), but does insist that they must form up in an orderly queue beyond the walls of the world of nations. In other words, the most speculative sciences must be furthest away. But what of the scientific knowledge that Vico says arises from within the world of nations? How is it different and special? It is different and special because it reveals the beneficial plan that God has put in motion by having the wheel of His creativity turn ours. Along the way, our ancestors had no clear sight of this ('That which did all this was mind, for men did it with intelligence; it was not fate, for they did it by choice; not chance, for the results of their always acting are perpetually the same.'[12]). But we are now in the happy position of being able to review how each phase has been laying the preconditions for the next – though without going on to become indigenous to it, as is the way with the smooth, Darwinian schemes of evolution. Let me now let Vico say all of this in his own words:

> Our Science therefore comes to describe at the same time an ideal eternal history traversed in time by the history of every nation in its rise, development, maturity, decline, and fall. Indeed, we make bold that he who meditates this Science narrates to himself this ideal eternal history so far as he himself makes it for himself by that proof 'it had, has, and will have to be'. For the first indubitable principle posited above is that this world of nations has certainly been made by men, and its guise must therefore be found within the modifications of our own human mind. And history cannot be more certain than when he who creates the things also narrates them. Now, as geometry, when it constructs the world of quantity out of its elements, or contemplates that world, is creating it for itself, just so does our Science [create for itself the world of nations], but with a reality greater by just so much as the institutions having to do with human affairs are more real than points, lines, surfaces, and figures are. And this very fact is an argument, O reader, that these proofs are of a kind divine and should give thee a divine pleasure, since in God knowledge and creation are one and the same thing.[13]

Giambattista Vico and *Inventing Socrates* – plus Homer, American Indians and Make-Believe

You will have gathered by now that I am using *Inventing Socrates* like a trope. Everyone knows that Socrates was condemned to die by his own people, the Athenians; and that he drank the hemlock cup. Everyone also knows that when Plato came to write the account of his trial and execution called the *Apology*, he chose to call him the 'Gadfly of Athens', in tribute to his life spent stinging the leading intellects of Athens into re-examining their beliefs. His practice of going after the assumed and the obvious through a series of innocent-sounding questions was both irritating and original – and we should note that these are the very qualities that are liable to have you strung up in any age, if you press them to the end! Over the course of his life, he made a lot of clever men look hasty and unprepared. It was also in the nature of his method that it undercut the basis of tradition and civic religion. When the question 'Why?' starts to be asked, these institutions are normally the first to fall. 'Because our fathers did it this way, and theirs before them' is not an answer that satisfies for long. This also explains why Socrates was a hit with the young men of Athens. The technical term for his method today is the 'Socratic elenchus'. It was irritating because it played on the distance between the concepts of everyday language, though specifically the function of predication, and (what we can now call after Vico) the creative intentionality of the human speaker. When asked what some quality is in itself, we tend to slip that responsibility and stand instead like kings of creation and point to examples of it: namely, 'I declare that it is this, or this, or that.' The Socratic elenchus worked to expose and humiliate this slipping. It was original because if objects of intellection can exist qualitatively in themselves, rather than in the aeons old way of mechanical substitution ('War is a god'), then you had opened up the possibility that knowledge could be a concrete quantity that might now be achieved far more substantially than ever it had before. Plato would take this to its maximum in his intelligible World of the Forms, but it should now be obvious how thrilling Socrates' style could be to sincere young people – thrilling as a gold strike, because it seemed to prove that there was something actually there to be mined. And it is always young strong people who rush to gold strikes, heedless of the risks. Here is a short example of the elenchus in action between Socrates and Euthyphro:

> *Soc*.... just at present I would rather hear from you a more precise answer, which you have not yet given, my friend, to the question, What is 'piety'? When asked, you only replied, Doing as you do, charging your father with murder.
> *Euth*. And what I said was true, Socrates.
> *Soc*. No doubt, Euthyphro; but you would admit that there are many pious acts?

> *Euth.* There are.
>
> *Soc.* Remember that I did not ask you to give me two or three examples of piety, but to explain the general idea which makes all pious things to be pious. Do you not recollect that there was one idea which made the impious impious, and the pious pious?
>
> *Euth.* I remember.
>
> *Soc.* Tell me what is the nature of this idea, and then I shall have a standard to which I may look, and by which I may measure actions, whether yours or those of any one else, and then I shall be able to say that such and such an action is pious, such another impious.[14]

I introduced the concept of *Urstoff* at the end Chapter 2 in relation to the Presocratic Thales and his belief that water was it. I have used it already in this chapter in relation to Vico's belief that the human mind is 'code-bearing', unconsciously written through with the part that it will play in the plan of the 'ideal eternal history'. And now I have let it describe also the ultimate goal of Socrates' elenchus. Because human life must go on; and more to the point here, because it did go on before philosophers came on the scene; humans have always had to posture like 'kings of creation' – or if you like, naming things like Adam and Eve were originally charged to do. We have seen that Vico grasped this inescapable constructivism. And we have observed for ourselves that there can be no other way with human animals. In the excellent explanation of Aristotle,

> Language serves to declare what is advantageous and what is the reverse, and it therefore serves to declare what is just and what is unjust. It is the peculiarity of man…that he alone possesses a conception of good and evil, of the just and the unjust, and of other similar qualities; and it is association [in a common perception of these things] which makes a family and a polis.[15]

Humans don't just squawk and bark: they have been freighted from the off with a communication system that only activates itself at the ethical level. Like all animals, humans are relentlessly moving towards ends. And like all animals, these ends may be as discernible as the fly is to the lizard. Or they may be more rhythmic and seasonal, and indiscernible. In the case of the human animal, however, discernible and indiscernible ends may be said to correspond to the conscious and unconscious states of being. It is as though, when he is conscious, man has to create a narrative from the materials he finds around him, in response to which he can be instinctive. Yes, it is as though he tries to ape the seamlessness with their environments that the other animals enjoy; but because he has himself constructed the environment with which he will now attempt to merge, he begins the existential existence which it is the human animal's peculiarity to endure. He is both king and subject; and he must take responsibility for both sides in the balance. When he tries his best to achieve a seamless integration with the narrative he has constructed, when he falls into a trance at a tribal dance or when like the ancient Egyptians he gives his gods human bodies and beasts' heads, we call it early, primitive and naive. But we forget that it was the impulse to locate and then designate good and evil that called him to act this way; and that language and art followed as the means to bend others to join him beneath the arch and terror of his narrative. For example, when you go walking today with the Bushmen in Namibia, and it is a hot day under the sun, you will see that they move completely silently and impassively. As you follow their wise example, you will doubtless play the scientist on them and applaud them for how they are saving energy and moisture in a barren landscape. But ask them why and they will tell you that the sun is watching from above, and that if he sees you down below chatting and enjoying yourself, he will assume that you like his heat, and turn it up a couple more degrees for good measure. In that little scenario, you, present-day you, play Socrates. You do what he did for the citizens of Athens. Like him you see that all word formation from babies on up is the attempt to classify. This is the reason why all languages, once established in their patterns, can be reduced to lexicons: why all histories can be reduced to natural histories: and why finally all religions can be reduced to science. They just need someone who can come along and help them to lose their innocence and come of age. And in every case, the questions will always be of the sort that Socrates asked. They will gently expose the imprecise way that language has up to then been applied to reality; then they will push on to try to coordinate it on stable quantities of meaning.[16] Socrates still imagined that that coordination could mean that the traditional life of justice could be matched to the pure intellection of its principles, and defended against the relativism of the Sophists; and Plato then explored what that would look like as an eternal blueprint for an ideal republic. Today in the West, it is less fashionable to follow this line, and more fashionable to match the inborn ethics of language to what Wikipedia represents, and to think of good and evil in terms of those who are for or against the progress of the species in mind and body. But my point is that either way, Socrates emerges as the hero and icon of Western self-esteem. He taught open-mindedness, come what may; until eventually what came to him was intolerance and small-mindedness and the charge of having corrupted the youth of Athens.

> Well, what do the slanderers say? They shall be my prosecutors, and I will sum up their words in an affidavit: 'Socrates is an evildoer, and a curious person, who searches into things under the earth and in heaven, and he makes the worse appear the better cause; and he teaches the aforesaid doctrines to others.'[17]

So the trope of *Inventing Socrates* supports a number of different viewpoints, which I will list now in the order in which they have appeared in this book. (1) It supports the self-esteem of the moderns over the ancients. (2) It supports the complementary idea that that self-esteem must have had an historical starting point on the human timeline – the idea of the Presocratics and of mental evolution. (3) It supports the qualifying idea that history is not divine history, but inevitabilities of cause and effect just waiting for the bigger picture that will show them for what they are – Cornford's thesis that Greek religion graded imperceptibly into Greek science. (4) It supports the possibility that though this happened, it was divinely planned – Vico's position. And finally, (5) it supports what I have been saying, which is that Socrates is neither ancient nor modern. If Western self-esteem is like a gigantic Zeppelin, he is like a hole pierced right in the middle of its fabric. And through him is escaping all of its airs and certainties. Everything on the timeline either side of him is rushing out through it. When I think of *Inventing Socrates*, I think of him as someone who did not follow the script. The script came into being from within time with the Presocratics, so that now we encounter it as something that has turned all time into a history that can be approached critically, through the sequencing principle of progress. Socrates professed to have no aptitude for theophanies of the gods or the crude natural philosophies of the Presocratics. He felt that these neglected the reasoning powers of the human mind and kept it craven and secondary to the world about it. He wanted to upset this balance of powers and repopulate the city of Wisdom with real and actual people.

> I must first know myself, as the Delphian inscription says; and I should be absurd indeed, if while I am still in ignorance of myself I were to be curious about that which is not my business. And therefore I say farewell to all this; the common opinion is enough for me. For, as I was saying, I want to know not about this, but about myself. Am I indeed a wonder more complicated and swollen with passion than the serpent Typho, or a creature of a gentler and simpler sort, to whom Nature has given a diviner and a lowlier destiny?[18]

But while this makes him the icon of perspectives today like secular humanism, and rightly so, his own natural horror at committing himself to paper, and paper's evidence, is that hole in the Zeppelin through which everything is whistling away. Plato did what he could to patch it. He wrote up the principal accounts of Socrates that we have today, as well as giving them their forward-thinking valence. Think of it like this: If Socrates had never existed, but philosophy had nonetheless been born and developed in the way it historically did, and the search was on for the missing link between natural and ethical philosophy; and if various cultures of the world were putting forward their claims, but the West as yet had none; then one of us today might well be tempted to invent the life of Socrates. In just the same way that Piltdown Man was invented by an Englishman in order to wrestle the mantle of the 'dawn of humanity' from the Germans and the Spanish and the French – so that Winston Churchill could write of these primitive Britons that they were the 'lords of creation'. And I suspect that our invented Socrates would look exactly like Plato's Socrates. And I suspect that Socrates foresaw all of this and understood its motivations. I suspect that he intuited that the human experience of life has forever been the experience of facing off against one's future biographer. Yes it is possible to abnegate this responsibility to do battle, and sink into ennui and the status quo. But when one rises up in a determination to be a personality, and knowable, the blood that one feels in that flush of oomph is warm and fluid in relation to how icy cold and inflexible is the pen and its page. Your lovers and friends knew you and you surprised them all the time with your freedom of thought. But in your biography you have become, just, inevitable. And do not forget that the other part of being human is to know that we play both parts in this at once. We demand freedom: and yet in our intellectual activities we become the means to the enslavement of others. Plato loved Socrates: *and was his biographer*. Of course not all of us get to have an actual biographer and a dedicated book. But rest assured that this is more than made up for in the biographies of the superorganisms in which we all participate. Perhaps you were just a hidden member of the working class. Fear not: you shall have your book of it. But let me give you now an example of why Socrates never wrote a jot himself, and left it all to others and Plato instead:

> I can not help feeling, Phaedrus, that writing is unfortunately like painting; for the creations of the painter have the attitude of life, and yet if you ask them a question they preserve a solemn silence. And the same may be said of speeches. You would imagine that they had intelligence, but if you want to know anything and put a question to one of them, the speaker always gives one unvarying answer. And when they have been once written down they are tossed about anywhere among those who do and among those who do not understand them. And they have no reticences or proprieties towards different classes of persons; and, if they are unjustly assailed or abused, their parent is needed to protect his offspring, for they can not protect or defend themselves.[19]

It is as though we must all live as the healthy carriers of our incurable disease. To live as an individual, to live, as I put it at the close of Chapter 1, as a 'soul radiating outwards', is to live in self-denial – is to live in denial of the facts. Writing, as Socrates decried it, is a perfect metaphor of this. It turns life and blood, and the possibility of those two giving you an extempore answer back, into 'solemn silence'. It turns them into immovable fact. As we grow older, the accumulation of facts becomes harder to resist; right the way up until the crown fact: death itself. Here, the soul is said to be extinguished, and switched out like a light. We are taught that there is nothing, in truth, beyond the grave.

We may choose early on to join the side of the disease in us. This will be called being realistic. And there is a kind of triumph with starting from the apparent certainty of the fact of death, and making it one's premiss, working back at people still committed to self-denial. When I said 'no more doctrines, and peripeties, and schools of thought', this is what I meant. These were the dynamics that I hoped to use to show what really happened with the Presocratics. Every human is a microcosm of the universe itself. We all contain portions of the supernatural and the natural. There are no theories, like evolution, that belong outside of us. We did not come into this world to line up and die and prove them right. Theories as attractive as the multiverse theories must be taken into us where they belong. In their case, there is no doubt that the theoretical journey into the quantum of all things truly does bring us out onto the possibilities of mass production and variety; for the quantum of all things would not be what it is, were it not as indiscriminate and promiscuous as to allow these parallel hypotheses. However, logic tells us that mass production and variety, the indiscriminate and the promiscuous, must be allowed to stretch to infinity; whereas the indignation of the human spirit rises against being dispossessed by such an unintelligent ruse. The scientist in all of us hides behind his spectacles and says, 'Try me, I am blameless, nothing will stick!' But he is after the God-particle, and zealous, so that self-denial will mean denying him and discerning his intention, which reminds me of this moral anecdote from T. E. Lawrence's *Seven Pillars of Wisdom*:

> Nasir rolled over on his back, with my glasses, and began to study the stars, counting aloud first one group and then another; crying out with surprise at discovering little lights not noticed by his unaided eye. Auda sent us on to talk of telescopes – of the great ones – and of how man in three hundred years had so far advanced from his first essay that he now built glasses as long as a tent, through which he counted thousands of unknown stars. 'And the stars – what are they?' We slipped into talk of suns beyond suns, sizes and distance beyond wit. 'What will now happen with all this knowledge?' asked Mohammed. 'We shall set to, and many learned and some clever men together will make glasses as more powerful than ours, as ours than Galileo's; and yet more hundreds of astronomers will distinguish and reckon yet more thousands of now unseen stars, mapping them, and giving each one its name. When we shall see them all, there will be no more night in heaven.'

'Why are the Westerners always wanting all?' provokingly said Auda. 'Behind our few stars we can see God, who is not behind your millions.' 'We want the world's end, Auda.' 'But that is God's,' complained Zaal, half angry. Mohammed would not have his subject turned. 'Are there men on these greater worlds?' he asked. 'God knows.' 'And has each the Prophet and heaven and hell?' Auda broke in on him. 'Lads, we know our districts, our camels, our women. The excess and the Glory are to God. If the end of wisdom is to add star to star our foolishness is pleasing.' And then he spoke of money, and distracted their minds till they buzzed all at once. Afterwards he whispered to me that I must get him a worthy gift from Feisal when he won Akaba.[20]

Ancient and modern, East and West. When the East rounds on the West like this, it is devastatingly effective, until there is nothing more to say, but acknowledge its superior romance. By a single flick of the will the prejudice of the home and the hearth destroys every book of science. The romance of the desert stars at night destroys those books. When you think about it closely like this, it is very strange that it does. Telescopes don't lie; and seeing is believing. Yet the denial of their disease – self-denial – in favour of the supernatural and God returns us instantly into a healthy possessiveness. Ancient and modern, East and West, Child and Man, Left and Right – yes, these must all be taken inside of us where they belong. This is not my idea, either; it is simply what I have always taken the author of *Ecclesiastes* to mean when he wrote: 'All *things come* alike to all':

> For all this I considered in my heart even to declare all this, that the righteous, and the wise, and their works, *are* in the hand of God: no man knoweth either love or hatred *by* all *that is* before them.
> All *things come* alike to all: *there is* one event to the righteous, and to the wicked; to the good and to the clean, and to the unclean; to him that sacrificeth, and to him that sacrificeth not; as *is* the good, so *is* the sinner; *and* he that sweareth, as *he* that feareth an oath.[21]

Since Eden, and since sin, men have been working out of the premiss that this is a universe of events – events of which it is possible to predicate their truthfulness or falsity from the point of view of existence, or of their having actually taken place. Either side of this 'actually', which may be impractically discreet to a coterie of witnesses, the methods of deduction and induction allow for others at a distance to believe in it – to believe in it up to and including the probability of fact. However, because sin involved believing the devil's lie that man would come into the quantum of all things *specifically* through a knowledge of good and evil, the Boolean predication of truth and falsity within a universe of discourse is not innocent.[22] In fact it has become the very emblem of Adam and Eve's original loss of innocence; plus the technical answer to how that loss of innocence is transmitted congenitally to all the rest of us. When the scientist says 'Hand on heart I mean *true*', he means *good*. When he says 'Hand on heart I mean *false*', he means *evil*. The human fixation on knowledge is not spotless wonder: it has this moral dimension. For example, a fiction may properly enough become one of the counted events in the universe in its inventing and telling in time. It may well have happened that a man called Socrates told of how the Delphian Oracle had instructed him to 'Know thyself'. His telling of it to others would have entitled it to the status of a fact – namely, of the order 'I swear that on such and such a day, Socrates said *that the Delphian Oracle told him...*'. But over the course of time, the moral, postlapsarian dimension of knowledge becomes apparent in how all such 'fiction events' become censored and replaced with non-fiction edits of the same event. 'Of course the Oracle didn't *actually* say that. Socrates was probably chewing magic mushrooms when he went in to consult it. Or better still, that whole story is something we know only through his biographer Plato's say-so!' With one of those deft little moves we all know so well, the Socrates of Plato's say-so becomes separated from the historical Socrates. That is how it is done; and we are all guilty, at some point, of having done it to someone. The collective effect of the violence is what I referred to in Chapter 1 as 'a charge sheet levelled at the human race along its entire length'.[23] Except the author of *Ecclesiastes*, he hasn't done it. 'All *things come* alike to all' – here he is exposing the international conspiracy to censor events. He says that we '*are* in the hand of God'. He says non-fiction can't reach back through history and censor the events of the soul and the supernatural. He says there is no timeline at all, but just one desert and its night sky, and God's grace to allow it that we may freely choose to flick East or West beneath it. Those stars have shone the same for everybody; we are the ones who can switch on or off like lights. 'All *things come* alike to all.'

The dynamic comparison between my approach and Vico's works because he is so firmly committed to the idea that universal (disembodied (dispossessed)) Western rationality cannot be the constant in history. God is the constant in history. The thought experiments of classical political philosophy that would have us re-enacting the original bartering and contracting of our forbears may seem to prove that the principles of social justice are as axiomatic as those of mathematics, but the rub is that there exists hard linguistic evidence that disproves this. This linguistic evidence that must be reckoned with is what Vico finds being reproduced in human nations at their primitive stages everywhere – 'the American Indians would now be following this course of human institutions if they had not been discovered by the Europeans'.[24] For him, the constant in history is therefore the intelligent design of God as it can be read like a clock from the creative productions of the pliant human mind. If you go into the jungle tomorrow and discover a lost tribe, and if you apply Vico's New Science, this clock is what you will find ticking. As you are at 5 pm, these people will still be at the early morning; but that you can find yourselves on the same clock-face is what will prove that you are both human, and that there is a benign God. And this, of course, is where he and I must start to peel apart. For the problem that I must immediately have with all such relativity theories as this is that they strip out the magic – where the magic is never something that I believe should be stripped out. All supernatural happenings may be shown, in the end, to have made causological use of natural parts, but that is no reason to lay the parts out on a table afterwards and say that that is what really went on. To reference the beginning of Chapter 1: any man may naturally align himself with any woman, and out of that produce children. But that is not a reason to take a man's wife away and give him another. Nor do we still react well to the idea of eugenics programmes or breeding farms, however sound their final results for the future of the species. Magic is unreasonable. Magic is love. Love is invisible. All relativity theories take up positions until they can triangulate on magic; then they destroy it by exposure to the light and replace it with a constant, sufficient to which all things can stand in relation. Vico was right: the ancients were sublimely poetical in their attitude to life. They exhibit simplicity's impulsive impressionism – and when you compare that to where we are today you get a story and all the shades of grey. When you add in the element of Divine intelligence, you get a template that the philologist may brandish against the philosopher's 'eternal reason'. The magic that Vico triangulates on and destroys is the 'eternal property' of ancient poetry – which he describes as the 'credible impossibility':

> It is impossible that bodies should be minds, yet it was believed that the thundering sky was Jove... [This] upsets all the theories of the origin of poetry from Plato and Aristotle down to Patrizzi, Scaliger, and Castelvetro. For it has been shown that it was deficiency of human reasoning power that gave rise to poetry so sublime... Hence it is Homer's privilege to be, of all the sublime, that is, the heroic poets, the first in order of merit as well as in that of age. This discovery of the origins of poetry does away with the opinion of the matchless wisdom of the ancients, so ardently sought after from Plato to Bacon's *De sapentia veterum*.[25]

Let us recall that in its own way, my discussion has passed through Homer, American Indians, as well of course as children and Make-Believe. But always in order to demonstrate that the poetical and the esoteric are not a juvenile form of answer. To the contrary, I think that they are everywhere and always versions of THE question – where that question begs an answer from beyond all the conceivable universes of discourse. The universe of answers is ripe and game for Vico and all other constructivists to use it to denounce all merely speculative knowledge. If the business of human life is to live by answers obtained in the here and now, then the quality and ambition of those answers becomes irrelevant – dangerous, even. Because answers in the here and now are able to generate their own methodology that is obvious and auto-mechanically coherent. In his lecture 'On Practice', Mao Tse-tung put it that –

> If you want knowledge, you must take part in the practice of changing reality. If you want to know the taste of a pear, you

must change the pear by eating it yourself...That is why the 'know-all' is ridiculous. There is an old Chinese saying, 'How can you catch tiger cubs without entering the tiger's lair?'[26]

I think this quote from Mao Tse-tung helps to bring out what Vico does that I do not. I don't believe that humans ask questions in order to receive answers – at least to receive answers from fellow humans. And I correspondingly believe that this accounts also for why humans who have been able to give inspired answers have so often been translated to the status of demigod or god.

This has become a completely self-regarding world, in which all questions have been stigmatized as metaphors for the past, and all answers have been stigmatized as metaphors for the future. For all that Vico does correctly with regard to the ancients, he still belongs firmly in this scheme, which I think shows itself clearly in the final quotation that I want to give to him:

> Hence poetic wisdom, the first wisdom of the gentile world, must have begun with a metaphysics not rational and abstract like that of learned men now, but felt and imagined as that of these first men must have been, who, without power of ratiocination, were all robust sense and vigorous imagination. This metaphysics was their poetry, a faculty born with them (for they were furnished by nature with these senses and imaginations); born of their ignorance of causes, for ignorance, the mother of wonder, made everything wonderful to men who were ignorant of everything. Their poetry was at first divine, because...they imagined the causes of the things they felt and wondered at to be gods. (This is now confirmed by the American Indians, who call gods all the things that surpass their small understanding. We may add the ancient Germans dwelling about the Arctic Ocean, of whom Tacitus tells us that they spoke of hearing the sun pass at night from west to east through the sea, and affirmed that they saw the gods. These very rude and simple nations help us to a much better understanding of the founders of the gentile world with whom we are now concerned.) At the same time they gave the things they wondered at substantial being after their own ideas, just as children do, whom we see take inanimate things in their hands and play with them and talk to them as though they were living persons.[27]

Of magic and men

Magic is everywhere, and everywhere it is being felt – has been felt – as our alter ego's revolutionary mood. We know who we are. We are necessity's children. Necessity is the city that we have built which is now bullying us. As I called the situation out a little earlier, we live as 'king and subject'. As subject, we enter into our revolutionary alter ego. And I think this is why in the twentieth century, and again now, the city and its functional accomplishments can bring on the artist in us, the magician in us. I think this is why so many young people of thought and feeling have been turned over to their better selves whilst walking the streets of cities. In nature and the countryside, you walk through a state of perfection that you can admire, but may not touch. The city, on the other hand, is your rightful blank canvas; and you may most definitely touch it. Necessity built your city and explains its habits to you now. But magic takes that flat reality and vivifies it and works it up into what I call THE question. Let us not fall into the intellectualist trap of believing that the existential life is one that is lived in solitude, by the mind apart. The traditional genius of existentialism has been to work and develop the truth that most all of the claims of objective morality can be gazumped by something more urgent, more pressing and ultimately irresolvable on the terms on which it accosts us. This is that our existence, which is everything for us, was triggered in time by someone else's finger. Not ours. Further: existence implies *none existence* – or the time before our existence, in which we were not. The existential point of view, once under way, clearly implies that this 'time before our existence' is of infinitely higher rank than our present state. That it is of infinitely higher rank because it was the time in which the almighty decision to shoot us into existence was taken. The retort to this mystical language, which goes that it was nothing so much as the haphazard of a man and a woman getting together and the sexual act, does nothing against what I am actually saying here. For what I am actually saying here is that the existential point of view works out of the juxtaposition of existence and pre-existence – but really, out of the obviousness that the latter is in every sense superior to the former. Once we accept this, the existential agony of a human life then becomes the fact of having to live with that knowledge. It becomes the fact of having to *pretend* that one can be a meaningful wilful creature after facing such a crushing proof of one's eternal insignificance. Existentialism shows that the human mind is stricken by the two operations that it has to perform over and again in sequence. The first operation is to acknowledge that the absolute definition of existence would be to have power of choice over life and death. The trigger finger. The second operation is to acknowledge that we really are free in relation to this faculty of volition that we have that can turn its back on the sensible and reasonable and do truly outrageous things. You could say that the whole history of Western philosophy is an attempt to make terms with these two operations and their sequence. To try to live totally free and crazy is to find yourself condemned in a thrice by the mores of your age. To relent and go over to the side of the mores of your age and objective morality is to live in the land of the absurd, in which institutions wield laws as though they were God – in which they arrogate to themselves the power of choice over life and death. And yet you know already by the first operation that this power truthfully resides in the land of pre-existence, into which no human mind could venture and survive. Could venture and exist. In this way, existentialism shows itself to be exactly what it has been: both atheism's and theism's most uncompromising voice, and the confusion of that. All of this is summed up succinctly in the words of Georges Bataille:

> If I think of my coming into the world – bound up with birth, and beyond that, with the union of a man and a woman, and with the moment of that union – a unique chance decides the possibility of this self that I am; indeed the wild improbability of the mere being without which, for me, nothing would exist. The slightest change in the series of which I am the term, and instead of myself avid to be myself, there would only have been some other, and as for myself, there would have been only a nothingness, as complete as if I were dead.[28]

So yes indeed, we are necessity's children. For want of a better word, that is, we are necessity's children. We come into being as simply the latest (greatest) part in a rational series. Thus begins our death-struggle with rationality and the logical structures of the world around us, and with which we share the materials of our bodily being. As we have seen in this book, this world and our place within it can be understood rationally; while the documented history of that understanding is what we then learn to understand, in turn, as the progress of the species, and the final justification of everything. But we have also explored how this very dogma can be regarded as our deadliest enemy – and yes, how there is an element in traditional existentialism that gets this for what it is. For it shows how different we are to all the other creatures, insofar as we have it in us to live stubbornly and disobediently in an irrational and eternal parallel universe. This parallel universe is of course the universe of our pre-existence, which we can only inhabit by seeking to act irrationally in this, the present universe of our actual existence. All children do this naturally, without having to think about it. The mature philosopher has to knit his brows and relearn how to be a child all over again. To be free would be to have the law and all corresponding objectivity spool out as the irrational tilts of one's will. To be free would be to choose the moment of one's birth and death. And for a while, as kings of their lands called Make-Believe, children come close to accomplishing this. But something that existentialism has never coherently explored on its own behalf is the extent to which the capacity of this species of ours for wilful irrationality implies a prior existence. Not traditional existentialism's 'nothingness' of pre-existence, but a whole other world – that parallel universe – in which we actually *were* once upon a time, and whose behaviours can be remembered by us now and sought for again in sensation and emotion.

Think of it, if you want, like the escapement in a mechanical clock. The existence of each of us, our individuality and personality, is in a constant death-struggle with mechanical friction. This mechanical friction stands for that whole way in which rational understanding uses knowledge to make comparisons between us – comparisons whose eventual purpose must be to terrorize us into a single, sexless being. This mechanical friction is intent (hell-bent) on driving us through gate after gate of the same homologating question – Margaret's question in Goethe's *Faust* – 'And I who thus could feel – am I the same?'[29] Here is the question that looses the better part in each of us into the worse part in some other, some observed other. Always that way around, by the way – always the better into the worse. Because that is what humans do – from Plato's analogy of the cave to Stockholm syndrome, it's obvious that this is what humans do. Like the pendulum fighting against friction, we undergo this struggle between who we uniquely *are* and then who we are *categorically* as members of the species (of which we are daily fated to know ever more). So why hasn't friction won yet, and the pendulum stopped swinging? The answer, as with mechanical clocks, is the escapement. In a mechanical clock, the escapement takes energy from a source external to the system (a coiled spring or a suspended weighted) and transfers it to the pendulum or other such timekeeping device. In our case, the escapement is the projecting energy that produces the lands of Make-Believe and all their variants. The traditional questions of existentialism could never have been produced by a human brain in a vacuum, though this is the image that is usually suggested by their alienating, disconsolate results. They are produced by our innate conviction that the world of our pre-existence is more ontologically real than this world of our actual existence. The energy of this conviction overcomes all the known bastions of necessity which this world can present us with, or that we can impose upon ourselves. Water, air, fire, earth. Concrete, steel, blades and bullets. The wilds of nature. The streets of the city. Philosophy may pride itself on having arrived on the scene as man's first true solace: as the wise man's escape from religion and blabber, pleasure and pain. But no: its questions all arise because we cannot but look at a rock or a cloud or a street sign, and see a face. I remember that great line from Louis Guilloux's semi-autobiographical *La maison du people* – the line around which that whole tale seems to shimmer and ache. The shoemaker protagonist Quéré is described by the narrator, his son, as knowing the habits of his city and its quarters so well that

> *Il connaissait les habitudes de la ville. Il savait, en écoutant le sifflet des locomotives, si le temps serait à la pluie.*
> He knew, listening to the whistle of the locomotive, whether it was pulling in the rain.[30]

Here we encounter a classic example of the nexus between social realism as art and existentialism as mood. The nexus comes about because from the one side, social realism is always seeking for an *Urstoff* beneath the tinsel – I mean how it looks to the under classes of society as representing the physically real of life. To depict them is to cut through the airs and illusions of the upper classes to the tragic and the repressed. To change them would therefore be to change the very structures of human life itself. Then from the other side comes existentialism, comes philosophy itself. And what it supplies is the fitting mood, because that mood is all that it can supply in the end. In the under quarters of the cities (the places to which all real artists are at some time drawn), the man of our times lives out the primeval truth of his condition. He finds that he lives within inanimate structures that confine and direct him. The rock of the cave has become the concrete that looms over him now. Thus the first act of the human condition is lived and relived in post-industrial cities – and being lived and relived, it defies every pretension of the progress of the species. However, because he knows deep down that this miserable existence is the poor relation of some pre-existence, he is able to feel the magic of his pre-existence, and against all the odds he is able to impose it on the very same structural necessities that he knows he can never change. Hence the tragedy of the nexus. But a beautiful tragedy. And the reason why I say that philosophy – even when it is at its most beguiling in Descartes' *cogito ergo sum* – is not the salon or the study (or any such versions of self-sufficiency).

Philosophy is the language of the difference between existence and pre-existence. The material world is the world of your death, for it contains things that can kill you. Out of this it shrieks its claim to be the only reality that there is. But because you are a human, you know that your death belongs to your life, which in turn belongs to the world of your pre-existence, and its choice which made you. The reason why we come across fragments like Guilloux's, in which the steam locomotive – that emblem of the industrial age's steel and roar – is worked into a cosmogony so that it is said to 'pull the rain', is because as humans we are driven to defy existence. Yes: this drive is our escapement. OK: of course it is just a train, made of material things for a boring and functional purpose. And if you stand in front of it on the tracks, it will run you down. But when we work things like trains into books as art we do what Guilloux did, and re-describe them in cosmogonical ways. It is our way of trying to surmount every imperative that existence presents us with.

Does this mean that when he wrote those lines in 1927, Guilloux produced an authentic Presocratic fragment? Yes it does; of course it does. It also helps to explain why the first philosophers chose to write their art over all the known places of the *physical* world.

Almost all of the educated talk about the antagonisms between science and religion, or between science and the humanities or just between science and anything else persists today on the logic that science is competing with everything else out there for the single glorious mantle of 'truth'. Consider the following from Steven Pinker's recent article, 'Science Is Not Your Enemy':

> We know, but our ancestors did not, that humans belong to a single species of African primate that developed agriculture, government, and writing late in its history. We know that our species is a tiny twig of a genealogical tree that embraces all living things and that emerged from prebiotic chemicals almost four billion years ago. We know that we live on a planet that revolves around one of a hundred billion stars in our galaxy, which is one of a hundred billion galaxies in a 13.8-billion-year-old universe, possibly one of a vast number of universes. We know that our intuitions about space, time, matter, and causation are incommensurable with the nature of reality on scales that are very large and very small. We know that the laws governing the physical world (including accidents, disease, and other misfortunes) have no goals that pertain to human wellbeing. There is no such thing as fate, providence, karma, spells, curses, augury, divine retribution, or answered prayers – though the discrepancy between the laws of probability and the workings of cognition may explain why people believe there are. And we know that we did not always know these things, that the beloved convictions of every time and culture may be decisively falsified, doubtless including some we hold today...

As for literary scholarship, where to begin? John Dryden wrote that a work of fiction is 'a just and lively image of human nature, representing its passions and humours, and the changes of fortune to which it is subject, for the delight and instruction of mankind'. Linguistics can illuminate the resources of grammar and discourse that allow authors to manipulate a reader's imaginary experience. Cognitive psychology can provide insight about readers' ability to reconcile their own consciousness with those of the author and characters. Behavioral genetics can update folk theories of parental influence with discoveries about the effects of genes, peers, and chance, which have profound implications for the interpretation of biography and memoir ...[31]

It could not be better put than this. Science has always been right about everything. It is just that we have had to work hard to make science come towards us. 'Science' is a word that means the whole truth; and scientists eagerly anticipate the day when we shall see the whole of its whole. Pinker is entirely right. He is as right as that if you stand in front of that train you will get smashed. And just in case the non-scientists try to mount a counterargument to the effect that there are aspects to human flourishing that science just can't touch, we all know what the answer to that would be – survivalism, or self-preservation. That is what links this species of ours to science's knowledge. This is the suppressed premiss from which Pinker (and all like him write). It is the premiss that no-one in their right mind would want to stand up and get smashed by a train. They would be mad to freely choose that. The only way that science could cope with their decision would be by uncovering mitigating circumstances of some kind or other. But the idea that you would cheerfully get up on a bright day, and place yourself in the middle of the tracks: no, science cannot enter with you into that place. It can only have you consigned to the Mad House instead.

Why can't science join you in that place? We now know the answer. It is because that place is the place of your pre-existence rather than your existence. The place of your existence is where science is lord and master of all. It is the place of everything that Pinker has listed that is true. In the place of your existence, fire burns and water cools and there really is no God. Stand in front of the train and pray all you like and it will still smash you. Deep down, everyone knows this. However, in the place of your pre-existence, the place from whence you came and to which you will return, nothing that concerns existence is of the least bit important. How could it be? Any pebble on any beach has a more explicable career in existence than you. Scientists can work out its geological age; then from its mineralogy go on to trace all the different elements that went in to making it as far back as they like. They can also go as far forward into the future as they like and determine what it will be reconstituted as. But in our case – the human case – it is different. In our pre-existence, none of us chose to be born and live, which fact gives the lie at once to the premiss of survivalism. Survivalism, if it were true, would describe the madness of standing in the way of science – the way of the train. And surely everyone who has felt the twist of mortal fear attests to that? And yet it and the whole notion of advancement rolling forwards with the ages *is* wrong. It is wrong by virtue of the sheer fact that we have it in us to resist it. The other animals don't. But we do.

You see, there is nothing juvenile in going Presocratic like Guilloux did. He took the steel of a train, and gave it a soul, and made it pull the rain. And now look what Thales did. He took the lodestone from Magnesia in Ionia[32] and did exactly the same:

> Thales, too, seems, from what they relate, to have supposed that the soul was something kinetic, if he said that the (Magnesian) stone possesses soul because it moves iron.[33]
>
> Aristotle and Hippias say that he gave a share of soul even to inanimate [lit. *soulless*] objects, using Magnesian stone and amber as indications.[34]
>
> And some say that it [soul] is intermingled in the universe, for which reason, perhaps, Thales also thought that all things are full of gods.[35]
>
> Will any man who shares this belief bear to hear it said that all things are not 'full of gods'?[36]
>
> Thales said that the mind of the world is god, and that the sum of things is besouled, and full of daimons; right through the elemental moisture there penetrates a divine power that moves it.[37]

And here is what it all comes down to. This thing that Thales did doesn't date him. You do it all the time. (Do you own a boat: have you given her a name?) The truth that science knows it knows has nothing to do with what it means to be human.

What it means to be human is to stick two fingers up to science and truth. Right until the bitter end. No other animal can do the inexplicable and end itself. Science and truth tell you that, and they're right. When other animals end themselves it is always in the name of territory or power or courtship.

If it were possible to somehow give to a non-human animal the guarantee of not dying by hazard or natural causes but living forever in this place of its existence, do you not think it would choose to live forever? If Darwin tells us that everything has all along been about survival of the fittest, how else could it choose? In fact when you see it like this, you understand that it is hardly a sensible question at all. You have questioned the very law of nature itself, and asked it to skew from the straight – and of course it won't! There is no story to be had here. But now if we put the question to a human animal, it is all so very different. It becomes a story, it becomes a book, it becomes the essence of art itself. I wouldn't want to live in this place of my existence forever. I may even choose to exit it very soon. And I could do that tomorrow, should I wish. It is these elements – the element of the free will and the element of two fingers to the truth – that allow us into the authentic way to read the Presocratics.

The truth says: 'Thales and the Presocratics did it like that, but I would have done it like *this*.' But then that is exactly what the truth would say, because it has no understanding or desire of magic – magic, the wondrous wilful stuff of human dreams. Of human dreams that cannot be broken because they were only ever fantasies in the first place. Because that, as we know, is the logic of a fantasy: that it belongs to that place of your pre-existence. Your wife can never be your fantasy because she belongs to your existence. It is only ever the *other* woman who can be your fantasy. So, for example, your wife could for a time be the fantasy of some other man looking on. But never yours. From out of your fantasy you could make art; indeed, *you should make art*. But any art you make won't be the image of your wife.

Science knows that it *is* the truth: and in any other situation that would ensure it of the victory. But what science doesn't realize is that it is up against fantasy. And for me, it's fantasy every time.

Here it is then: Thales and the Presocratics knew exactly what they were doing. In just the way that every human being knows exactly what they are doing in the moment of their choice. Here it is then in all of its exhilarating strangeness: Thales might have just as easily produced the truth of today; or the truth of the sixteenth century; or even the truth of 100 years from now. As long as he was a human he might have done that. Every time that you hear science trying to say to you that you are in its thrall and purpose:

that you will only ever get to know as much as the age in which you live: remember to stick two fingers up to it. What the human mind can do in this age it could have done in any other. So please don't confuse 'education' with human genius. The evolutionary theory of human intelligence teaches you that every age puts its understanding into books and schools and universities, so that it can be worked upon and improved by succeeding generations. This is why white Europeans are the best and every brown face in a jungle deserves the right to an education; while the safeguard worked into this from whiteness' point of view is that no amount of education can ever change a person's colour. Africa will always be Africa, and Europe will always be Europe.

I say instead that there are geniuses in the jungles and the savannahs, just like there are geniuses ploughing fields in Europe. *Who* gets educated in the end is as random as the lottery, yet it determines the very concept of evolution which says that the arrow of progress points forwards, and that you will obey the limitations of your time and place and hold to your appointed station.

I don't want any of it.

To say, for example, that there is something linear and cumulative between Thales' philosophy and its religious pre-history is plain wrong. Or between Thales and his pupil and successor Anaximander, plain wrong again. The logics involved in this are simply incompatible, for they are the logics of truth on the one side – and then on the other, of originality, or genius or whatever you want to call it (though by now you know exactly what I mean). The logics of truth tell you plain face that Anaximander *was* Thales' pupil and successor: that like Thales he was a citizen of Miletus and the younger of the two men. All of this and everything that follows from it is true.

But what has the truth to do with mankind? If in some future utopia, men and women could act only in accordance with the truth, in other words in accordance with Wittgenstein's one and sublime 'book of Ethics',[38] then that would at the same time be the end of men and women. What the West calls 'truth' is really a statement about temporal succession. It is also why the place of pre-existence is eternal and unknowable. The eternal and the unknowable can only be performed by men and women as art, language – as communication itself. It is therefore always a stage, while the truth is always the audience looking on.

I don't believe that there are any distinctions to be made between the members of this race save than that of this distinction between the stage and the audience. The role of the audience is always played by the numerical majority, and what they eventually see through to *is* always right, *is* always true. But for that very reason it can then bear no logical relation to what was originally performed. Because remember, the performance was a fantasy – and no weight of the truth can ever break fantasy's dream!

The weight of truth says that Anaximander could not have come before Thales as much as Thales could not have come before ancient religion. Or of course, that Socrates could not have come before the Presocratics. Yet the fact of the matter is that these temporal successions belong to the left-to-right of syntax – that is to say, the syntax of survival, by which all material things of animate *and* inanimate being *become* the truth by persisting in their forms. We more readily apply this understanding to animate things, because the beasts of the field show us by the efforts they make what it means to persist in life and existence. But even a rock of the same field would show it to us. All because it is customary to say now that (thanks to Thales and the first philosophers themselves) the stable meaning of our idea of rock (relative to the catalogue of meanings of other things) is the same thing as our left-to-right sense of its unchanging *Urstoff* (and whatever we choose to think of that as being). In fact, if you take the truth into its most abstract worlds of the mathematical equation or the logical proposition, you will only see this more clearly still. You will see that your pen is only permitted to move forwards across the page as long as that forwards movement is exactly congruous with the preservation of some *thing*. The thing itself could be anything – a quality, or a quantity. The vital factor that creates the forwards movement is the continuing sensation of the preservation of *it*. This is why, to the Western mind, the truth has come to mean the same thing as the world of our existence. When we say 'seeing is believing', this is what we mean. But all of this is administered and controlled by those in the audience, whoever they may at any one moment be – and the identities of those on the stage or in the audience are going backwards and forwards and swapping all the time.

Like Thales, Anaximander also went down in his own lifetime as legendary in practical ingenuity and traditional wisdom. Like Thales, then, he was one of those who lived his life up on the stage.

And like Thales, the principal dates for Anaximander are somewhat speculative. Scholars are reasonably content that he was in his early sixties around 540 B.C. We should not then think of him as being that much younger than Thales. Diogenes Laertius has preserved a summary of his achievements:

> Anaximander son of Praxiades, of Miletus: he said that the principle and element is the Indefinite, not distinguishing air or water or anything else... he was the first to discover a *gnomon*, and he set one up on the Sundials (?) in Sparta, according to Favorinus in his *Universal history*, to mark solstices and equinoxes; and he also constructed hour-indicators. He first drew an outline of earth and sea, but he also constructed a (celestial) globe. Of his opinions he made a summary exposition, which I suppose Apollodorus the Athenian, also, encountered.[39]

From the audience's point of view, there is little question that Anaximander's genius unmasks the preceding genius of Thales. If it were not for Anaximander (they say), we would have no perspective from which to look back and historicize the maverick statements of Thales about water. By declaring that the 'principle and element is the Indefinite', rather than any some particular thing, Anaximander was reaching up towards the principle of which water was merely one of its innumerable possible declensions in the lower orders of thought. This highest principle was the principle of rational necessity itself. Thales had stopped the storytelling of myth and religion dead in its tracks by introducing the idea of a trace element. Stories operate according to their own strict rationality; and we have seen that science refuses to believe them because it points out that the premises upon which their rationalities build are fabricated and fictional. Any viable trace element would, by contrast, be empirical and non-fictional. However, none of this insight would have come down to us (N.B. as the audience of) today were it not for the fact that Anaximander took up with Thales' magic and worked out how to explain its trickery. He worked out that Thales' magic was working with our heart's ready-made fixation on necessity, on rational necessity. If the processes of the universe are not random or chaotic but traceable, then lurking beneath the sum of them all must surely then be the prospect of some gigantic necessity – for let us not forget that human understanding is not the same thing as the understanding of a computer or any such artificial intelligence, however complex. Human understanding is indistinguishable from its accompanying emotion – an emotion that no soulless machine can ever replicate. This accompanying emotion is the hope that fact will ultimately give way to spirit. Revealed monotheism has in this respect always seemed too easy a solution. The fully maxed-out human understanding seeks a pact with the devil. We are back with Dr. Faust, though this time Marlowe's:

> I have been more acute than all these triflers,/Doctors and authors, priests, philosophers;/Have sounded all the depths of every science...Therefore to magic, with severe/And patient toil, have I applied,/Despairing of all other guide,/That from some Spirit I might hear/Deep truths, to others unrevealed,/And mysteries from mankind sealed;/And never more, with shame of heart,/Teach things, of which I know no part./Oh, for a glance into the earth!/To see below its dark foundations,/Life's embryo seeds before their birth/And Nature's silent operations./Thus end at once this vexing fever/Of words – mere words – repeated ever.[40]

Here we get a chance to see further into this curious dynamic of the stage and the audience: and why it is essential that we are made aware of it today. The scientific deconstruction of stage-magic is propelled by the secret desire to have an even deeper, more occult magic.

And in Anaximander's example we see this very clearly. A stage magician himself, he was soon after made into Thales' audience (and just like Thales was soon after his own death made into religion's audience). The fantastic trick of the *Urstoff* was something that Anaximander was said to have explained on the principle of a necessity intuited from the observable difference between disorder and order. When I say that science hungers after the occult of the spirit beyond the fact, this is what I mean. Through the organs of sense, the human mind can take cognizance of limitless impressions. But everything that we include within the meaning of the word 'understanding' implicates us in the belief that all disordered impressions are hanging breathless on their final reckoning. Thales' water works its magic upon our minds by awakening within us our primal desire to see this reckoning made. Time, change, chaos and flux are the stuff of the limitless impressions made upon us: yet they cannot affect the fundamental operation of our understanding, which remains aloof of this mess, and knows itself only through its ability to penetrate to everything's essential nature. Thales' water lets us feel this power of ours for the first time. This feeling is the magic of his stage-show. But we can only say this now because Anaximander followed him – Anaximander who showed all of this to us by situating Thales' achievement within his own strange vision of our modern-day physics.

Take the following account of his vision from Simplicius, which includes an original quotation from Anaximander's writings. Notice the qualifier at the end involving 'retribution' and 'time'. It should remind us of no less the second law of thermodynamics.

> Of those who say that it is one, moving, and infinite, Anaximander, son of Praxiades, a Milesian, the successor and pupil of Thales, said that the principle element of existing things was the *apeiron* [indefinite, or infinite], being the first to introduce this name of the material principle. He says that it is neither water nor any other of the so-called elements, but some other apeiron nature, from which come into being all the heavens and the worlds in them. And the source of coming-to-be for existing things is that into which destruction, too, happens 'according to necessity; for they pay penalty and retribution to each other for their injustice according to the assessment of Time', as he describes it in these rather poetical terms.[41]

Let me give it to you like this: Imagine a stage-magician today performing the usual run of tricks – sleight of hand, mechanical illusions like sawing a lady in half and so on. Now imagine being in the audience, but equipped with none of the modern conceptions of cause and effect. In other words, with none of the thoughts that make you absolutely believe that what your eyes are seeing cannot actually be happening because behind the evidence of sight must be some science or other. A rational explanation. Human history has always had magicians on the stage and audiences in the stalls. In fact this arrangement has fairly dominated our history until comparatively recently. Until the beginning of what this book is about. Men like Thales have always been the magicians, learning the ways and techniques that get things done unexpectedly and ingeniously. They have been among the world's sages, prophets, heroes and priests. Sometimes in the pay of kings and those who have needed their magic to get ahead. But sometimes on their own. But what about the stalls? What about those in the audience amazed and applauding? For it is these – the majority – and how their mental equipment has changed that is the story of Western philosophy. It is often said that the birth of Western philosophy was the birth of the great age of Criticism; and that this is a continuing age, in the sense that what we are presently living in and our attitudes of mind represent its most advanced stage. What changes in the sixth century B.C. is that those in the stalls are given the new garment (yes, like a new fashion) of a thing called science, or rational explanation. So that you no longer go 'Ooh!' when magic is performed, and say afterwards that the spirits were at work. You go 'Ha!' and talk afterwards about how clever it all was, and how behind it all must have been smoke and mirrors. When post-philosophical critical man is being magnanimous today, he says, 'He really took me in for a while, you know. He really did.' In the dark ages of the time when pre-philosophical man was being magnanimous, he used to say: 'Here is something great that I could not have imagined being done. WHAT DOES IT MEAN (AS A SIGN)?'

Dream songs

It all comes down to the question of value with which I started this book. With human value, or self-love. Or the difference between the world of emotion and dreaming and the world of facts, unalterable facts and the left-to-right arrow between facts – or time and the second law of thermodynamics. If you ask it of a good Stoic like Seneca, you really get it plain and hard:

> They are mad who lay at the door of the gods the cruelty of the sea, excessive rains, and the stubbornness of winter... It is not because of us that the universe brings back winter and summer; rather these have their own laws by which the divine plan operates. We have too high a regard for ourselves if we deem ourselves worthy to be the cause of such mighty movements.[42]

We have statements such as these because we have no other way of accounting for human genius – or indeed for the many subsets of human genius, of intuition, inspiration, extemporization and imagination. Between the religionists and Thales, then Thales and Anaximander, are voids which admit of no valency in any direction. For almost the whole of human history, these voids have not caused any bother; but to post-philosophical critical man they are the biggest bother of all. For almost the whole of human history, men sought merely physical, material and genealogical superiority over each other. But then in ancient Greece (which is simply the example chosen for this book (and therefore this same book might be written again, in time, from any number of conceivable perspectives)) something changed and men sought for intellectual superiority over each other. Now the voids could become bothersome. They could become bothersome because in truth there never have been any relationships of dependency between individual manifestations of human creativity. And that there never have been is because – as I have been arguing – there is no real competition between the truth that science *knows* and the reasons why humans make-believe. Humans can become less human and more scientific, yes; but there is no amount of science that will ever replicate the tiniest human dream. That is to say, what humans can attain to knowledge of, factually speaking (and by now we know the answer), is the knowledge of their predestination. The most perfectly knowledgeable human conceivable would be a perfectly silent creature because he would have nothing left to say. He would be more silent even than the non-rational animals, who must still yelp their pleasures and pains. He would know the truth about such sensations and remain impassive to them. But this has not yet come to pass and we still have dreams and dream songs. And while perfect factual knowledge points at the world of existence to prove itself, dream songs laugh in that world's face. Yes: that is all the use they have for existence.

When one human mind creates something: when it utters even just a single word: the whole of everything is contained within that word. What the word is in itself is irrelevant. The only thing that matters is that there is no other animal on earth that can utter a human word. And don't talk to me about parrots, because I am not talking about the human word's imitators. I am talking about how the whole of everything of what it means to be human is contained within each and every example of this unique thing that humans do. And then as we have been noticing all the way along this tale, there is this, too: that words joined to words making sentences of systems of understanding dehumanize us and extinguish us eventually. It makes for a very strange situation to be in. And talking about 'truth' doesn't help with it one bit. It doesn't because there is truth at both the extreme ends of the situation. At the one end, there is the truth that a human uttering even a single word is an authentic performance of everything that a human is in distinction from everything that a human is not. Then at the other end, there is the truth of what is really going on underneath that performance to make it possible – everything that Pinker's science would show. Every act of human expression up to but excluding that final extinguishing and silencing is symmetrical and identical in respect of its authentic performance factor – for each performance is repeating and screaming the single human denominator, which, as I put it earlier in this chapter, is to know that you are different and dislocated from everything else animate and inanimate. Just a soulful creature with no natural place of its own. This shared lament – this homesickness for a supernatural home – is what all human oral communication and artistic exhibiting has been about since the beginning of time. It only changes with the first philosophers of ancient Europe and the beginning of what I called the 'strange romance' in Chapter 1. We now no longer have a thousand and one charmed circles of use and wont, and no earthly reason to choose between them, but the first flush of science's one measure of truth. This is the end of symmetry in time and its love, transacted human heart-to-heart, and the beginning of the white man's unrequited love of the world. In putting the world under his magnifying glass (and learning back from the world how to make that glass ever more powerful), the white man hopes to become like the secret of its mechanism. He begins to lust after the elevation of the mind over the heart and the kindling of dispassion. In the Chinese *Book of Songs*, we read the meaning of the old symmetry (no left-to-right). There we read how the human animal is fixed with an immortal appreciation of mortality. The heart in us can love the heart in another. And the mortal ending of the blood-life of our lover's heart can send us into an immortality of grief. This is the only sense and knowledge that there can be. Immortal grief over a mortal heart remains the only predicate-subject function that we have. We are taught in school the opposite to this, that grammar is like the scientist's physics; and that just like the scientist's physics might one day become the tool that forges our brave new race, so grammar is ours to do with what we want. But this is not true. Any amount of grammar will only contain one lesson in sense and knowledge. This is that the sole meaning of humanity's immortal grief is flight from this world – in fact right the way back to our immortal origin. This possibility of flight is what permits the dreamer to dismiss the world and everything in it of existence. The more the world is opened up by knowledge to show what it ontologically *is*, the greater is his joy in dismissing it.

Yes: for as long as it is remaining true to itself, the human animal says the whole of everything that can matter to it with every little thing that it says. And here in a poem from the ancient Chinese *Book of Songs* is the whole of everything that matters to it:

Crossing the river I pluck the lotus flowers;/In the orchid-swamps are many fragrant herbs./I gather them, but who shall I send them to?/My love is living in lands far away./I turn and look towards my own country;/The long road stretches on for ever./The same heart, yet a different dwelling:/Always fretting, till we are grown old![43]

'The same heart, yet a different dwelling:' – or Ecclesiastes and 'All *things come* alike to all:' – Age after age this wisdom kept the symmetry in place. Between the great thinkers there were voids that were left as voids. And wisdom was left as eternal. But now in school we learn Criticism. And in our hands Criticism fills the voids with histories of transmission that are observed to run always left-to-right, ancient to modern. Thinkers are arranged into movements and trends and before we realize it that has become all that we know them as. We would do well to remember that the West's first philosophers birthed philosophy only because philosophy appeared to them to be the truer form of religion. There was no development, just the continuation of the story of humans doing what only humans do. I had occasion to mention the second law of thermodynamics earlier in relation to Anaximander; and now it appears it can help us again here.

The second law came into being because Western physics has no natural way of replicating the human mind's ability to think of only one thing at a time. This, by the way, is also my answer to why we will never have true artificial intelligence. The human mind is like a tube of Smarties from which only one Smartie may be extracted at a time. Whereas any worthy Western physics, be it quantum mechanics or Einstein's two theories of relativity, Newton's mechanics or even all the way back to Anaximander – all of these physics must be able to see every potentiality within their theoretical universes at any one instant of time (or not be a physics at all). Anaximander is recognized as an inventor of the physics of today precisely because he abandoned the one-at-a-time of whimsy and creationism to speak instead of justice and retribution. This is the idea that at just the same instant that something is on the way out then something somewhere must be on the way back. This is the idea that we know to recognize as 'eternal conservation'. One thing happening, and then another thing; and the mind that can only take them in as that order: here is a description of the human mind. One thing happening, and only to be able to log that it had happened because it could be identified with reference to some other concurrent happening; and the physics that can depict their relationship: here is a description of eternal reason [as an addendum we might note that when the ancient commentators looked for a miracle in Pythagoras' life, they looked for it in the idea that he had been in two different places at once: 'He was seen in Croton and Metapontum at the same time of the same day'[44]].

But here is the problem that brought the second law of thermodynamics into being. Justice and retribution and things on their way out and back and eternal conservation – well, there just isn't any whimsy or creationism in that. There just isn't an arrow of time. And that's a problem because it's only ever one Smartie at a time with us. The difference could not be more extreme or categorical. We experience life in a way that is cumulative and irreversible. And because this means that our life will be followed by our death, it cannot be ignored – even by physics. For we must not forget that it is in the nature of physics that it should, strictly speaking, ignore it. It looks through the eternal eye, seeing every objectively potential event in an equal glance. And these events are all that it sees, because of course it designates from the start what will be the integers of its seeing. And this, too, becomes the measure of its success and of all it looks to achieve. A good and worthy physics is adjudged to have uncovered the level at which elemental components of the physical world behave in a reciprocal relationship of absolute consistency with each other – one going out at exactly the rate as another one is coming back. Again: justice and retribution. So notice, then, that there is nothing cumulative or irreversible about this. When you jump from a building and hit the ground and die, there is always a conceivable level at which the process of your coming apart and dying would cease to present you with the full stop of your death. At that super-reduced level you would be looking only at problems of engineering; and we all know that what can be engineered can also be reverse-engineered. And yet we just do know that we experience life from left-to-right, and then die, and do not come back: so physics had to come up with the second law.

The first law deals with the pleasing observation that in quarantined and controlled thermodynamic systems energy can neither be created nor destroyed so that its sum total will remain constant. Anaximander's idea of 'eternal conservation'. This is the same level of analysis at which your body could be brought back to life – brought back to life because this level of analysis is totally and utterly *inhuman*. It is not cumulative and irreversible, where these are the very two traits that allow us to experience the normal range of human emotions from love to grief. The whole key to the attraction of Scientism is that it allows us to slip that empire of pleasure and pain and enter the soundless majesty of numbers. The mental activity by which you conceive a number (or a property) into being is quite identical with the stun gun vision of its constellations and the patterns that cannon between the numbers with no heat exchange or loss (or noise), because truly the holy mystery of numbers is that there really is something in each that retaliates perfectly on the same thing in the others. This guarantees that the cannoning patterns will go on to eternity, and we are beguiled. And from the youngest age. When we are taught to count, we go 'one' and 'two' [two ones] and 'three' [three ones]. Yet there is no way that all the number ones in the world can be identical and at the same time be sufficiently distinguished for us to count them out in a series. Our first lesson in mathematics is also therefore our first lesson in philosophy: and our first lesson in philosophy is, in fact, our first lesson in the difference between immortality and mortality – and in how every step of our human life will involve us in having to fudge the two as we never live clearly for either side. The second law of thermodynamics brings all of this back to earth and to the hot, noisy, accumulating world of human emotion. The second law is how science is made to come to terms (for now) with the fear of death: for notice that science's best shot against mortality is still to try to cool it all down cryogenically to suspended hope. The second law reminds us that if immortality *looks* like endless numbers and their reciprocating constellations, then mortality is still the only way that we can go about counting them. One Smartie at a time. Immortality just is; but counting introduces the idea of spontaneity. The second law states that an isolated system will automatically evolve until it reaches equilibrium. Furthermore, it stipulates that this evolution will burn up energy, so that such energy can no longer be considered to be available to the system. Physics uses the measure of 'entropy' to describe this increasing quantity of non-useful energy. An isolated system that has achieved equilibrium is said to be in its highest state of entropy.

Here we see that man, the counting animal, gives spontaneity to a world that wouldn't otherwise have the means to give it to itself. And then all the advantages of spontaneity – all the accumulating things like progress and evolution and our pride in both. Physics just shows you what is really, atomically there; and because it must always reduce to what is really, truthfully there, it can have no way at all of speaking into the questions of pre-existence and the questions of life and death. Any theoretical system that bases its veracity on an *Urstoff* is doomed to take its originators only further and further away from these questions. If you jump from a building and die, the *Urstoff*-understanding takes it all the way down through you to the worms in the ground that will eat you – then from them to worm-eating birds and out to the whole great scheme of the eternally conserved. The *Urstoff* is everywhere; it is directionless. And yet here is the super-weirdness of it all: only man, the stumbling bumbling counting animal can see it and praise it. Seneca was right: nature is wholly indifferent even to itself: and that is the final proof of how utterly perfect it is. It does not have a will to be self-conscious with; it is utterly incorruptible, which leaves us with the super-weirdness that it is only man, the wilful and corruptible animal, who can see it. But in order to see it, the mind of a man must each time make a beginning – 'one', 'two', 'three'; 'past', 'present', 'future'. The second law of thermodynamics has traditionally been the reconciliation between this and the *Urstoff*-understanding. Despite the timelessness of the latter, we really do observe events to move from the present into the future rather than from the present into the past. So we create a quantity called entropy that effectively allows us to continue to use the zero-sum game of mathematics, but at the expense of a universe which must be conceived to be a continuously expanding system. Entropy means that we are always running at an energy deficit which the expansion of the universe is assumed to make up.

Here is how it is. I said that every authentic human verbalization is symmetrical in time – is a single resounding truth, the same every time and clear as a bell. Well there is a parallel to that in the mathematical, *Urstoff*-understanding of physics, which is also symmetrical in time. And then there is how I said that what the West calls its accumulation of knowledge really is happening left-to-right – and how there is now a parallel to that, too, in the second law of thermodynamics. The second law imposes upon physics the fact that to the observing human eye, there is a natural and spontaneous preference in nature for events to unfold present to future (deficit to credit); notwithstanding the total absence of this preference at the unblinking level of atoms. Here has remained one of those intriguing openings that modern physics is yet to fully exploit: namely, the corresponding conclusion that if all of the above is fact, then what we have always called 'time' may simply be an exclusive feature of the observing human mind. My suggestion in relation to the Presocratics is that we make a direct comparison. All the dream songs that the human race has ever conjured up have been a jumble of nonsense, *save* for the single truth which they all cannot but contain. This is the truth that *homo fecit* 'man made it'. This truth doesn't undergo change or development. *Homo fecit* applies as equally and unmistakeably to Shanidar – our 100 000-year-old cave[45]– as it does to the Hadron Collider. And we know, additionally, what peculiar dimension *homo fecit* supplies, or projects. This is the moral, or emotional, dimension. As go the lines from our Chinese poem: 'The same heart, yet a different dwelling' [always the same single truth]; and: 'Always fretting, till we are grown old!' [its moral, or emotional, dimension].

For all time, this was how it went. Men and women counted and they walked, one foot in front of the other; and this forward momentum satisfied the inevitability that they wanted to ascribe to their customs and laws. The ancient Greeks had a word, *dike*, which would grow into its philosophical fullness of meaning with Plato's *Republic* and his promotion there of the 'state of being just', or *dikaios*. But long before that, it had enjoyed a less-contested career as referring simply to the historical precedent – or Way – of a people or practice. If we leave the European example and go east, bypassing the rupture of the Presocratics, we instantly pick up with the unbroken continuation of this phenomenon. As A. C. Bouquet and others have pointed out, you can trace the undying persistence of a mighty and irresistible Way – right the way from the *hodos* of the Pharisees to the Dialectical Materialism of the Marxists.[46] And yet what the Presocratics were able to discover appeared then as it does now to be as real and belligerent as time itself. If you are the cradle of civilization as the Greeks were, and you then have the fortune to combine that with the discovery of objective truth, then as sure as pride is pride you will be started on a course from which there is no return. For just as the second law is where the mathematical paradigm of truth meets the fact that a digested apple has already supplied a portion of the energy of its own transformation, the law of ancient and modern is where the dream song meets the fact that innocence can only be lost but never regained. No European can become a barbarian again, because entropy takes care of that. But the Barbarians can always be educated. You could not wish for it to be better expressed than in these lines from Xenophanes:

> There never was nor will be a man who has certain knowledge about the gods and about all the things I speak of. Even if he should chance to say the complete truth, yet he himself knows not that it is so. But all may have their fancy.[47]
> Let these be taken as fancies something like the truth.[48]
> Yet the gods have not revealed all things to men from the beginning; but by seeking men find out better in time.[49]
> If god had not made brown honey, men would think figs far sweeter than they do.[50]

Xenophanes was the first of the self-centred singer-songwriters when that was becoming the thing to be. Think of Los Angeles and Laurel Canyon in the late sixties, if you like, and the great revival that was going on there. In fact we may as well ask like Guilloux:

were they writing Presocratic fragments there too? He was born in Colophon, in modern-day Izmir Province, Turkey, sometime around 570 B.C. When the Medes captured the city in 546/5 B.C., he left it, taking his art to Sicily and Catana that we know of.

Xenophanes was a poet, but he wasn't just performing Homer anymore. He was writing his own lyrics, steeped in that unvarying mood of the troubadour. I'll sing you a song of something you'll recognize from your own heart: and if I can do that it will by definition be subversive of civilization and its chain gang coherencies: and that will also be its pull. *That* unvarying mood.

But here is what Xenophanes does from those lines above that is so here and now and everywhere. He separates proof from truth, science from the dream song. He says, 'All dream songs have only ever sung the same truth in the same way; yet quite what exactly that truth is we cannot ever know.' He says that it is an immemorial experience of the human race to know that what we call the truth comes home to us as nothing so distinct as a sigh or a mood; and that we congregate around the best music and song not because it captures the truth for us in nets, but because it is the only moment in which we can be still and watch the butterfly of it flutter past us and back across some vast ocean of regret – yes: back to the Garden. We are here, and what we call the truth is really this sensation of looking but not touching. But the spell can't last; and in the itch to understand what we have just heard, we panic and enter self-consciousness; and then we do the only obvious thing we can and turn to the physical world to try and make a logical beginning in its solidity of being. Xenophanes did this himself, of course – '… but by seeking men find out better in time'. He had observed fossils of sea creatures far inland of the ocean, and hypothesized that the sea must periodically take back the earth and return it to mud; and that having done so, and after a time, it then releases it so that it can rise again and dry out, and from there become the land of a new world. And from his line above about honey and figs, he references the contingency of proof on being. In a world of being that only included figs, they would have been the sweetest things. But that is what we call proof, while what we call truth is nothing to do with it, no. Proof is a land all of its own, perfectly coherent on its own logics. The truth is another whole land, its opposite. And as much as you could live out your whole life in the land of proof, you could live out your whole life in the land of truth. Except something has made it that you can't. You have to live in the land of proof and watch the butterflies fluttering back to the land of truth. You just have to stand there entranced and watch them go.

The other great singer-songwriter of those times was able to put it into two giant lines. I mean of course Heracleitus. He said that men are,

> Immortal mortals, mortal immortals,
>   Living their death and dying their life.[51]

The truth is immortal and the proof is mortal. The truth is the soul and the proof is blood. The truth is the soul and its proof is blood. The blood is of the earth and it is the blood in us that watches the soul flutter back across the ocean with the butterflies. Yet the soul misses its blood – would somehow die without it – and always comes back to it. There are drugs and things that can prolong its flight. But the next morning it needs to be back with its blood. Wants to be back.

Prison numbers

But first consider this: the imagination is the only part of us that can truly be said to 'wander'. Solitary confinement for long periods is the most effective way of breaking a man because of this. In the French penal colonies, the most violent and irrepressible prisoners were sent to *reclusion*; and it seldom failed to break them. In the cell, alone and in silence, the prisoner is forced to live the eternity of a full stop. He is dehumanized, and effectively made to be his number – prisoner 56435. On the other side of the world, at exactly the same time, a philosophy professor is being entranced by the idea of the eternal essences of numbers. That their essences never change. The number 56435 is the same everywhere to anyone who chooses to apprehend it. All Western philosophy deifies this changeless paradigm of truth – sighs for it. But at the same time, no one is feeling more God-forsaken and alone than prisoner 56435 in his cell. And what will in the end break him will be the fact that he cannot bear eternity – or the changeless perfection of his *reclusion*. The imagination will wander. And when the full stop is as small and filthy as a concrete cell, its wanderings either side of the cell will soon dwarf it: then swallow it completely. When they remove a man after five years of such wandering, and he is stark raving mad: this is what has happened to make him so. The judge said in condemning him: 'You will serve 5 years of timeless and eternal truth!' And the imagination recoiled and wandered and made past and future times of its own and filled them with things that were not really in the cell. And then a point was reached when those things became more real than the cell. And yet there are contemplatives – hermits – who seek out this existence for the whole span of their life, but do not go mad. There is a Russian proverb, formed in the time of the Gulags, which goes, 'In Siberia, men find God.'

It doesn't seem to me that anyone could really and honestly love God – that if God is all the traditional epithets heaped on Him by an adoring temporality it would be wrong to love Him anyway. That would be self-imposed *reclusion*, and I won't do it. How can you love eternity? How could you leave your blood behind and love it?

At this point we have to remind ourselves that we only have fragments of the Presocratics, so this is probably as far as we can push into them in our agitation. And we have to remind ourselves further that we have changed them from the men that they were into the bullets of the gun we are now holding to our head. The gun of numbers, eternity, *reclusion*. For all the rest to take place, someone, somewhere had to be designated the first born of Reason. That person was Thales, European and white. Since then, that is how we have calibrated all the questions and problems of human life. We have learnt to say that the questions and problems persist only so long as their protagonists remain to be educated into the sure-fire way of coping with the shock of brown. I mean: how *do you cope* with the shock that people from a different continent can be a completely different colour to you? And come on, you know just what I'm talking about. Just think of all the science fiction you love. Or just all the science you love. When one day soon we do discover creatures on another planet, do we want or expect them to be the same colour as us? No, we don't want that. No, that would be profoundly underwhelming. We want otherness and its terror: for that, after all, was why we started to use the word 'alien' in the first place. And when once we have discovered the green men, you can be sure that we will do to them what we did to the brown men of our own planet. We'll run a set of rudimentary tests to determine whether they really are 'intelligent life'. And if they succeed in passing those we'll then begin to implement our standard post-Thalean process for coping with their greenness. We'll say: 'Sir, I declare that I do not see your greenness but only your true and underlying numbers. Indeed, Sir, I declare to you the inestimable boon that by those numbers you may consider yourself just as (late and) great as us. Even more, Sir, I hope that one day you yourself may even find it possible to ignore your (repulsive) greenness. That will be a great day. The day which all good men anticipate with hope and longing. The day of true equality and democracy and... blah-di-blah.'

But the green man may well respond: 'My greenness betokens that I have a home on a planet that is not this one. I don't want your equality and democracy of numbers. I find your whiteness as incredible as you find my greenness. I am homesick and I want to go home.' [At that point they locked up the green man to stop him from escaping]

The proper way to read the disconnected lyrics of the Presocratics and understand what was really going on with them is to read them as men learning to put the gun to their own head. Don't try to dig for ways in which the one thinker might have influenced the other. Before them, the truth had nothing to do with words or propositions or numbers. Go right back as far as you dare – all the way back to the first humans, whoever they were. And I don't mean back to some primates grubbing around inside tree trunks with sharpened sticks. We have become far too accustomed to going weak-kneed at that sort of thing and whispering 'look, intelligence!' But we make fools of ourselves if we do that because no such thing can be an example of intelligence if intelligence is the quality that separates humanity from everything else. There will never be intelligent machines and there will never be intelligent beasts. But we can choose to say that there will be; and what is more, we can destroy our humanity in the process of trying to show it. All primate behaviour can be explained by Science and Darwin, and all human intelligence can't.

Human intelligence is deciding to stay in the cave when everything that has been written since has promoted the virtue of going out into the light. Alcmaeon (fl. early fifth century B.C.), the Presocratic who Theophrastus tells us was especially interested in the difference between human and non-human life, but for whom we have only the scantest of fragments, has left this huge line:

> For Alcmaeon declares that men perish because they cannot link together the beginning to the end.[52]

Everyone who subscribes to the virtue of leaving the cave must interpret this to be a criticism of the human condition; and then following on from that, to interpret it to be the call to found a new race that would join the beginning to the end in knowledge. However, I don't interpret this as a criticism at all, save, perhaps, of eternity. I believe that it is a mercy that men die – a mercy in view of what human intelligence really is. Go right back as far as you dare: now tell me what you see. You see the first humans. And what is more, you immediately recognize that they are humans because of their defiance and their two fingers. They exhibit that they are the intelligent animals by doing what no other animal can do: this is to give voice to the truth by shattering it against the rock of adamant that is the geological, flameproof world of numbers and law.

A painting on a cave wall when the time would have been better spent grubbing for food!

The only writings in which I have found the glory of man separated and distinguished from the laws of the universe are the Christian Scriptures. There you can read freely that the intelligence of man on earth exists within the span of his living and dying. At Revelation 21.5 you can read:

> I am the Alpha and the Omega, the beginning and the end.

This Alpha and Omega, this Christian God, is forbidden to the glory of man. Yes, men die because they cannot join the beginning to the end; but then dying is what men do. And laughing in its face is their glory. Science tries to join the beginning to the end and make men live forever. But as I said, take any word, any proposition or any number and shatter the truth against it. Do it because everything else is proof – proof for or against God. Everything else is just atoms or God. And this is where we catch the Presocratics – and indeed where they catch us. Whatever the truth is it is escaping from this world to some other. And the feeling that all true lovers come to associate with the truth is the lament of not being able to go with it. Yes: all that the glory of man can seem to do now is to shatter and explode itself against the adamant of Science, and then watch the shards flutter away.

I think all serious students of the Presocratics have always discerned that they are nothing but the collective fragments of a single mood. I say now that this is their mood. Before them, it is correct to say that the mood could not have existed. After them, it is correct to say that we have never left it. For there is just no turning back from thoughts such as these from Heracleitus:

> Of the Logos which is as I describe it men always prove to be uncomprehending, both before they have heard it and when once they have heard it. For although all things happen according to this Logos men are like people of no experience, even when they experience such words and deeds as I explain, when I distinguish each thing according to its constitution and declare how it is; but the rest of men fail to notice what they do after they wake up just as they forget what they do when asleep.[53]
>
> The sun will not overstep its measures, or else the Furies, the allies of Justice, will find it out.[54]
>
> Those who speak with intelligence must stand firm by that which is common to all, as a state stands by the law, and even more firmly. For all human laws are in the keeping of the one divine law; for the one divine law has as much power as it wishes, is an unfailing defence for all laws, and prevails over all laws.[55]

They pull in the opposite direction to his 'Immortal mortals, mortal immortals...' But together they make that single mood.

And again from Pythagoras: famous for putting harmony's numbers into nature:[56] something for our pride of mind:

> So Pythagoras turned geometrical philosophy into a form of liberal education by seeking its first principles in a higher realm of reality...[57]
>
> Life, he said, is like a festival; just as some come to the festival to compete, some to ply their trade, but the best people come as spectators, so in life the slavish men go hunting for fame or gain, the philosophers for the truth.[58]

But like us today he could be pulled in the opposite direction:

> Pythagoras son of Mnesarchus at first worked strenuously at mathematics and numbers, but later could not resist the miracle-mongering of Pherecydes.[59]

I want, however, to give the last word to Empedocles, because of all the Presocratics he was able to discern that what we know as human life is basically a thermodynamic event in which the ice-cold oblivion of our souls is being pumped through with the warmth of our blood. That pumping and warmth puts us into time, and enables us to love each other with all of time's uncertain hope:

For the blood around the heart is the thought of men.[60]

4

The Fatal Masks

When I awoke, hell burned within my brain,
Which staggered on its seat; for all around
The mouldering relics of my kindred lay,
Even as the Almighty's ire arrested them,–
And in their various attitudes of death
My murdered children's mute and eyeless skulls
Glared ghastlily upon me.

PERCY BYSSHE SHELLEY

Throughout this book I have tried to bring to light the certain and ineluctable relationship between the reductionist point of view and the idea of the ethical pursuit of progress. On the face of it, there is nothing in the one to suggest the other; it is difficult to imagine that an imperative to any sort of behaviour can arise from a belief in atoms and the void. And yet it is the case that time and again the one does slip inexorably into the other.

Suicide

The history of Western criticism is marked by thinkers who have stood upon the pulpit of empiricism and blasted into fiery hell all those who have dared not step into their line. And of course this is entirely apt; for the history of Western thought all told simply *is* the history of Western criticism. All of its great leaps forward are expounded as a criticism on some former benighted state of knowledge. So much so that the only way that you can successfully accommodate the Western concept of progress within a theory is to say that it is a 'privation theory of progress'. That is to say, its concept of progress seems to have no substantial existence of its own save its ability to throw each preceding age into a poorer and degrading light. And we must be realistic about how this is done. When the preacher in the pulpit of empiricism casts back, he has eyes only for the bedevilling traces of the spirit and the soul. These are what must be eradicated. Their eradication is progress. I have had occasion to mention Bertrand Russell once before in this book; now let me bring him in here for his standout part in this. Writing on the Fathers of the Western Church and the Dark Age that followed upon them, he posited that

> It is strange that the last men of intellectual eminence before the dark ages were concerned, not with saving civilization or expelling the barbarians or reforming the abuses of the administration, but with preaching the merit of virginity and the damnation of unbaptized infants. Seeing that these were the preoccupations that the Church handed on to the converted barbarians, it is no wonder that the succeeding age surpassed almost all other fully historical periods in cruelty and superstition.[1]

This is how they failed us. They did not stand up and make their appointed contribution to the great march begun with Thales. We must not fail to notice that this is a very high court from which to be blasted. In fact it is to be blasted from the very physics of the universe itself. And therefore the victory that is imagined is a total victory. For there can be no appeal in defence to anything higher than numbers. For numbers, as we know, never lie. Here we see in even sharper focus the relationship between reductionism and an ethical victory. And we see also – and this is why I am using Russell – that the victory lends itself particularly to the Anglophone language of paternal, colonial superiority. To not march with progress is to suffer from a self-generated weakness – from a lack of moral fibre and an unwillingness to selflessly do your bit. And quick as you like, these words can rearrange themselves into the questions that have always been hung on the non-European races: Are they up to it? Can they ever be? Will they run away at a loud bang?

Because this is a privation theory of progress, it is insatiably reliant upon being able to identify anti-empiricism in every preceding line. It is not that God ever dies: it is rather that He is liable to pop up in any unguarded moment. Here we learn something important. It has long been an implement of adult sophistication to acknowledge that the religious impulse is ubiquitous and by no means confined to the traditional arts of veneration. Its features might just as well be observed in a stamp collector or a football fanatic. Once this giddy spiral of comparison is underway, it can seem not unreasonable to suppose that it should provide for a full and satisfactory disclosure of the real story behind the most persistent religion of them all: Christian monotheism. When once you can reduce it to its human protagonists – and noting that scholars are now over the squeamishness they might once have felt about including even Christ in that group – then you have just the most famous example of weakness, fabrication and faith. Because the historical Christians were humans like us, they were really doing no more or less than we now do; except that we do it so much more bravely and better by science. This winning magnanimity, which can now be shown by the moderns to the ancients, is the thread that ties together the whole long story of the rise of Western critical thought since Thales. The winners can hold up their hands and shrug their shoulders and claim the neutrality and immunity of history-making. That grand project of making-plain was all that they were up to – and what can be more irreproachable than that?

However, in this book I have tried to write an intellectual suicide. I have tried to write history that really does kick out the stool from underneath itself. By criticizing the so-called birth of criticism, I tried to do this. I went to the Presocratics and tried to show that the discovery of reductive criticism is a nuclear harvest that irradiates and destroys everything. And wait for it: that it does this by actually aggrandizing and perpetuating the supernatural. Yes: this is why it is a privation theory of progress.

Let me explain it in terms that will now be familiar from this book. If everything is a story behind a story until we butt up at last against atoms, the indivisible truth of it all, then, by the same process of sanitization we must admit to having killed off the very independence of perspective from which all Western criticism operates. When the Presocratic project eventually climaxed on the atomism of Leucippus of Miletus and Democritus of Abdera, this became the problem that had to be faced. If the traditional distinction between soulful human life and inanimate physical nature could no longer be supported, so that instead of the mind's eye and its supernatural illumination one now had only to conceive of a congregation of 'soul atoms' squaring off against a congregation of other atoms, then the process of human perception and intellection had to fall from its high throne of mystery and to become only a kinetic business of collisions and reactions. Consider the following fragments from Democritus:

> Democritus says that of all the shapes the spherical is the most mobile, and that this is the shape of the particles of fire and mind.[2]
>
> By convention are sweet and bitter, hot and cold, by convention is colour; in truth are atoms and the void...In reality we apprehend nothing exactly, but only as it changes according to the condition of our body and of the things that impinge on or offer resistance to it.[3]
>
> Bitter taste is caused by small, smooth, rounded atoms, whose circumference is actually sinuous; therefore it is both sticky and viscous. Salt taste is caused by large, not rounded atoms, but in some cases jagged ones...[4]

It is not difficult to imagine what it must have felt like to make the leap that these men made and actually deploy this critical weapon on the conventional wisdoms of the day. In the catalogue of human smugness, the rush of iconoclasm is probably only matched for force of feeling by Schadenfreude's inner calm. But soon the deeper consequences started to emerge. If atoms mean that there can be nothing untouchable and irrefutable as it was once illumination's business to provide, then you should no longer be able to talk in the old languages of truth. But let us be clear about something here first. No human ever imagined that one set of eyes and a brain could ever be sufficient to surmount all physical restrictions of time and place and come into the truth of all things. The first humans in caves never imagined that. But in its place they certainly learnt to trust in the resources of the supernatural.

All-seeing spirits could be co-opted into effectively extending one's sight lines. In time, these extended sight lines could be collected together and made the song-lines of an entire people. It was this resource that Democritus and the Atomists did away with. It had led to a language of aspiration, hope, perfection and justice that could not otherwise have been formulated as an ordinate reflection on conditions in this world. And we must be clear about this. If your whole world and all its impressions is a bag of bent nails (as indeed hard realism tells us this world is), then there is nothing within the logic of that world to make you think of a straight nail. There is nothing within a universe of cosmic indifference to make you think warm homeward thoughts. You might respond to me with the logic of opposites and retort that a straight nail is exactly the thing that a bent nail ought to insinuate. But hear me now: I said, 'if your whole world and all its impressions is a bag of bent nails'. What you just now took for spontaneously occurring logic would never actually occur. It would never occur, because the mental jump from a world of bent nails to the dream of a straight one requires a conscious and inexplicable act of defiance. I say 'inexplicable' from the point of view of a Godless world of atoms. To be the first human to dream the straight from the crooked, the perfect from the imperfect, and the just from the unjust is to talk a foreign tongue borne in from another world: the supernatural world. When Democritus and the Atomists did away with this world, they found that they no longer possessed the right to speak of their own achievements as though they represented the indisputable truth. Attempts were made to overcome this by reinstating the possibility of a penetrating kind of intuition acting over and above the mere atomic spectacle – and which the Atomists could claim to have accessed pre-eminently. But this was hardly a satisfactory rejoinder. There is an amusing fragment attributed to Democritus in which the atoms 'speak back' to the all-intuiting human mind and remind it of its total debt to them:

> Wretched mind, do you, who get your evidence from us, yet try to overthrow us? Our overthrow will be your downfall.[5]

I repeat: the only reason that we can dream of straight nails is because we somehow and supernaturally overlap with the world of straight nails. And it is a different world to this one.

Down here it really would be all bent nails and nothing more were our minds to operate strictly and superbly within the limits that classical atomism prescribes. But let the truth be told: not one human mind has ever been in that stripped-down state. It has not because it is in the human mind's very definition that it should be ceaselessly communicating the sensation of living in overlap between the natural and supernatural worlds. The Atomists and all the Presocratics only went looking for Truth in the first place because their minds had already reached beyond the material world. This ability of the human mind to displace itself forward of the present state of knowledge and to call that distance the 'quest for truth' is the chief mark of our species. And into this vacuum we surge forwards with our new ideas and hypotheses. But seldom, if ever, do we acknowledge that this vacuum exists because of this ability of ours to displace ourselves into the realm of the supernatural.

Here we come into the full meaning of why we work to this day with a privation theory of progress. The sum of all there is to know is a withering root. Start out as far out from it as you like then persevere and sweat yourself all the way down to the dry truth of it. Propositions, down to atoms, down to numbers, down to whatever. This is not progress; it's actually like watching water disappear down a plughole. Or like walking yourself to a standstill. So what causes it to transmogrify into an ethical vision of the progress of the species? Put simply: it is the false impression that this realism has at last named and shamed all those suppressed premises to human thought. All those suppressed premises that were supernatural premises. All those suppressed premises that were to do with religion, myth and superstition. This is how the problem of the ancient world is always constructed. From the point of view of knowledge and enlightenment, the ancient world is the man who built his house on the sand. And now we don't have to do that. But I hope I have now shown that the basic programming of the human mind is the binary code of affirmation or denial of God; and that all thought that is recognizably human thought must be analysable in terms of this coding.

For example, a great part of our present confidence in denying God still goes back to the Logical Positivism of the first half of the twentieth century. This movement was able to show starkly and spectacularly that the native place of truth in human life was in worded statements that might or might not be capable of verification by the established methods of science. Before this turn, philosophy might have felt confident to roam everywhere, making statements about the gods and the emotions as much as about more ordinary fare. The effect of Logical Positivism was not to ban the former metaphysical and emotive statements outright but to perform the political manoeuvre of stating that they were meaningless – that they were private matters of subjective interest, quite incapable of being settled by the public standard of truth and fact. This public standard was scientific method. On the one hand, we might observe that this slick and fair proposal was naive if it imagined that the God-fearing portion of the species would be content to be told that their cherished thoughts were entirely permissible but invalid in the highest court. But on the other hand, we might go deeper than this and deploy the central contention of this book. Is not *any* and *every* assembly of human words – especially one expressing a scientific law – a meaningless statement?

We have seen that the Presocratics got something devastatingly right, and that this allows us to see in them the inception of our present state of knowledge. They intuited that what any human can conceptualize as the final and utter truth (and we can all do this) must always be seen to summit on the features which would mark it out from all other mere opinion and relativism. You can call it the One, or you can come up to the minute and call it the God-particle; and it really doesn't matter. What matters is the fact that it is perpetually escaping our manual efforts to pin it down to something distinct in this world. One of the longest Presocratic fragments that we have comes from Melissus of Samos, and it exemplifies like no other the tyranny of knowledge in its Western setting. Melissus correctly identifies two phenomena involved in the pursuit of wisdom. Initially there is the excitement of the new and unrecorded, or what we call the adventure of ideas and the freedom of expression. This is the first sense in which we become liable to think that words and grammar are guileless tools which we may take up or discard as we wish. For in order for pride to have its way we demand that our knowledge be ever increasing, and this demand propels us on to the conquest of the undiscovered and the corresponding generation of new labels and classifications for new things.

And one of its chief thrills is that we don't need to ask God's permission or help to pin a label on something. However, beyond a certain point, this outward spiralling plurality starts to do a strange thing. At just the point where our increase would seem to be endless, it stops spiralling outwards and begins to spiral inwards. This is the second of the two phenomena that Melissus noticed. For sake of convenience we might choose to call this the Darwinian turn. For after all, it was Charles Darwin who did this last and best in recent memory. It was he who drew the line for us between the savage and our civilized selves. Knowledge and its increase is fine and good and well, he told us, but a savage might just as easily travel and accumulate new impressions and give them names. No, this will not do; and in any case, it was never quite what we meant by the idea of the truth. The savage is content to proliferate names and to gawk and tremble before the largest and most sinister of his discoveries. But the sense in which we would like to lord the truth over him is to know that we have gone the opposite way and managed to decline all known reality from a single Noun. And we might add that if the savage came first in the timeline, and went his way, then what other way can we go if we want to be superior to him now? Here is Darwin's turn in his own words:

> When we no longer look at an organic being as a savage looks at a ship, as at something wholly beyond his comprehension; when we regard every production of nature as one which has had a history; when we contemplate every complex structure and instinct as the summing up of many contrivances, each useful to the possessor, nearly in the same way as when we look at any great mechanical invention as the summing up of the labour, the experience, the reason, and even the blunders of numerous workmen; when we thus view each organic being, how far more interesting, I speak from experience, will the study of natural history become![6]

In Melissus' fragment we are made to face the fact that this preference of ours to decline from a single Noun is something that, as I put it a little earlier, could not have been formulated as an ordinate reflection on conditions in this world. Melissus points out that these conditions can only be sufficient to overwhelm us with the facts of growth and decay and the problem of what William James once called the 'saddle-back' of time. The present moment, which we should think of as the natural home for all of our aspirations about stability of meaning, is really not a place which we can ever logically inhabit but only a vantage point from which we look backwards and forwards.[7] And yet in spite of this 'continuous sensation' of our past, present and future,[8] we do harbour a strange dream of a place not terrorized by past and future. A place in which the first-person psychological experience would be the same thing as eternity – and therefore a place in which reality, or being, would be the equal prerogative of everything. Here we arrive at the sore crux of the human condition. From some other long-lost world we have retained the illusive vision of *being*, of *essence* or of *substance*. Aristotle's definition of it is justly famous and stays close to the original complexity of this situation. Substance, for him, is something that is taken to be able to be the subject of various properties; for he takes it that in order to talk sensibly, we would prefer to be able to penetrate through the endless varieties of sensory experience and cluster our predications around certain fixed flagpoles – flagpoles like 'man', 'ball', 'dog'. Yet the same logic that makes this entirely sensible at the same time disbars 'substance' from actually being any of the predications that cluster around it. For what we and Aristotle mean by substance is totally unambiguous: it is the *single* quality of existence that every existing thing displays *equally*. So here comes the sore crux. This supernatural conviction that we bear about with us is at exactly the same time at dagger-odds with how we should like substance to reflect well upon us. It is at dagger-odds because the latter is a superimposed wish, while the former is the truth. It is a truth that we receive as a spiritual gift and which allows us to see through the sea of happenstance to the convergences deep below. To the single convergence deep below. However, to see to this single deep convergence is the same thing as to become silent and dispossessed. You cannot enter into that inky calm with things in your pockets. This is the sense in which I claim that all human assemblies of words over and above this silent place are technically meaningless. Note: it wouldn't be like this in the *other* world, from which our notion of eternity and substance and truth came in. But in *this* world of time, this *reductio ad absurdum* is exactly what happens. One truth leads down to a deeper truth, then an even deeper one – and all the way down to silence. And no, this is not how we like it to go. We like to fill our pockets with things, with knowledge. We want to talk and burst with it. We want the spiralling outwards collection of labels. So really we want substance *and* plurality. And note again that the only reason for this is the pride of our race. Melissus thought that the only way to accommodate substance and plurality in a single conception was to determine a way of seeing reality at the microscopic level of identical atoms. And by the way, he didn't just foreshadow us; he foreshadowed also the Atomists of his own day. Here are his words:

> If there were a plurality, things would have to be of the same kind as I say that the One is. For if there is earth and water, and air and fire, and iron and gold, and if one thing is living and another dead, and if things are black and white and all that men say they really are – if that is so, and if we see and hear aright, each one of these must be such as we first decided, and they cannot be changed or altered, but each must be always just as it is. But, as it is, we say that we see and hear and understand aright, and yet we believe that what is warm becomes cold, and what is cold warm; and that what is hard turns soft, and what is soft hard; that what is living dies, and that things are born from what lives not; and that all those things are changed, and that what they were and what they are now are in no way alike. We think that iron, which is hard, is rubbed away by contact with the finger; and so with gold and stone and everything which we fancy to be strong, and that earth and stone are made out of water; so that it turns out that we neither see nor know realities. Now these things do not agree with one another. We said that there were many things that were eternal and had forms and strength of their own, and yet we fancy that they all suffer alteration, and that they change from what we see each time. It is clear, then, that we did not see aright after all, nor are we right in believing that all these things are many. They would not change if they were real, but each thing would be just what we believed it to be; for nothing is stronger than true reality. But if it has changed, what is has passed away and what is not has come into being. So then, if there were a plurality, things would have to be just the same nature as the One.[9]

I want us to be crystal clear about what I mean by all of this. The thesis of this book is that the supernatural is the only proof of the natural that we have.

I have talked a lot about fiction and non-fiction in this book and let me now bring all that talk to its ultimate conclusion here.

Replaced by machines

Once it has attained to the age of reason, every human life issues in a choice: the choice to go either in the direction of non-fiction or fiction. The two directions could not be more starkly opposed. The direction of non-fiction is a ready-written way. It is represented by everything that I have said concerning the human mind's ability to see a perfect likeness of itself in the substance or ontology of the universe. I have now explained that if this is the honest goal of Western wisdom, then its final satisfaction would render all wordage quite meaningless: for there would no longer be any distance of manoeuvre and dissent between us and this mad truth. And I have also explained that this truth would do away with time and its mercies: because this goal of Western wisdom is on its very logic – yes – 'ready-written'. To conceive it is to conceive also that it is a spell-binding doom, wholly without sweat or graft. It just is and always has been. In the Christian Scriptures, this doom is explained to be God Himself – although we should recognize that Christianity overcomes this problem by pointing out that Christ incarnate presents us with the opportunity to love a humane and fleshed out Truth. We should recognize, additionally, that were it not for this innovation, Christianity would have an impossible time of defending itself against the criticisms of the intellectuals. And fair criticisms they would be too. For as I have already pointed out, the gift of being alive to ghosts and our haunting is something that is every human's possession by right. Everyone is free and fitted to conclude that there could be such a thing as ultimate and final enlightenment, and that were we to come into it, we would call it Truth with a capital 'T' and raise it above all materialism. But by the same token, this universalism means that all religions and philosophies that claim this mantle can only be considered equal in respect of this fact. In other words, the fact of the supernaturalism of the human soul is not sufficient to raise one set of beliefs above the others. And we notice that this is because this statement is in the first instance a statement about the quality of humanity and *not* the nature of religion. On this point we encounter the basis of the vexed relationship between Western Christianity and the artists and the intellectuals.

Beginning with the intellectuals: it must be plain from what I have just said that if you give *insufficient* regard to how the humanity of Christ coordinates on the emotions of our flesh, then there is very little to prevent you from concluding that Christianity was just another religion put together out of the spare parts bin of the world soul. The method of historical-critical scholarship makes this inevitable. For the first move of this method is to declare that one shall not begin with anything connected to the haunted air. Thus you never investigate spiritual phenomena by investigating spiritual phenomena. No, you go instead to the next nearest empirical starting point. In the case of spiritual phenomena, this is now always human psychology and anthropology. The tacit understanding here which no one dares to challenge anymore is the understanding that spiritual beliefs are simply juvenile examples of problem solving – lingering bad habits whose total eradication would mark the dawning of a brave new age. OK: so you go to the human case and construct a catalogue of human requirements and then match those to their apparent fulfilment in the religions. This gives you a neat classification of religions. And when once you have armed yourself with this classification, there is now nothing to stop you from noticing the similarities and borrowings between the world's great religions; and then to feel flushed with your understanding and to write smart books about it. Within the Western tradition, Christianity has naturally enough been the religion subjected most of all to this treatment. And the conclusions that have followed have been what one might expect. Christ apart, it is almost impossible not to begin to see Christianity as a phenomenon grading imperceptible into everything either side of it. In fact, this grading *has* to occur if our scientific classification of religion is to hold up. Still the most epochal expression of this from a Western intellectual must be Friedrich Nietzsche's claim that Plato was a Christian before Christ.[10]

Now turning to the artists, and again we must emphasize, *Christ apart*, we have the problem of the 'glory of man'. This glory of man is represented by the choice that a human life may make to go in the direction of fiction. What do I mean in this context by 'fiction'? Well, if the doom of becoming non-fiction is that one gets so perfectly into step with the ready-written storyline that one loses one's prior sense of alienation in time, then the boon of becoming fiction is that one regains that and even amplifies it. Here we link up with the opening manifesto of Chapter 1. A world of fictional human beings is far preferable to a world of non-fictional ones; and don't the artists just know it! So much so that the idea that one would choose instead to dissolve into one's shared substance with God is what always repels the best of them in the end. It is *la guillotine sèche*. It is to disappear entirely and brutally into one's moving parts. This is not the glory of man. Let me give you now the most potent example of how we are, and should be, fictional beings.

For this I need a human experience that holds out the very real peril of collapsing us into those moving parts of ours. I find it in sex. Let me put it this way: think of that rational self-determination, that poise and pride that I have identified to be Socrates' place in our psyche. His stylized bearded image on books and posters. When we think of ourselves adoringly in this light, we think of ourselves as the animal that alone can live within its inner places, in a wordless sensation of its past, present and future. A dog would wag its tail and give itself away, but we the rational animal can consider our ultimate interests away from our moving parts. Unlike the non-rational animals we therefore live out our lives in visible *and* invisible dimensions. In the visible dimension we can look at each other and see the mechanical comings together that the plain fact of our parts makes possible. And I mean by this more than just associationism. I mean how we can go the whole way together in thought before even a word has passed between us. And I mean how this is in fact what should always happen in this world when a man and a woman meet. I mean that the first instant should be full and utter consummation; and I mean it because this is the law that is written into our moving parts. And like all law it is designed to be the enclosure in which subsequent freedoms may take place. When a man and a woman meet and recognize that they are a man and a woman, their story begins at the very end's climax. What unfolds next is a regression from the ultimate act. For into the moment come the actual considerations that determine how they will in fact go on to know each other. The place, their ages, their personalities, the proprieties and so on. It is as though they were rising from their shared bed naked to meet each other for the very first time. To lay it out like this helps to explain why human sexuality remains to this day our species' most emblematic problem. The fact that we can follow the logic in our moving parts out to their compatibility with another's – and do it in this back to front way – is the basis of all known perversity. For when you think about it, all known perversity occurs because it is mechanically possible; and like all sexual possibilities, that possibility exists ahead of it, written into the laws of friction, fluidity and thermodynamics. As much as Science's understanding of the moving parts of the universe makes its innovations and advancements possible, so too does its understanding of the moving parts of the human animal increase the range of that animal's perversity. None of which should surprise us, because (as per the point on which I began this chapter) to collapse into the moving parts of a situation is the same thing as to have given oneself already to their left-to-right conclusion. It becomes an ethical, or even an ideological, *fiat*. It is because we see the kettle already boiled that we have so much confidence in the application of heat to water. However, I began this by saying that a human life can choose two go in one of two directions, and if that was the non-fiction direction, then let me now give you the fiction, our invisible dimension.

Consider this: we don't just do things; we do things and then we try to interpret that doing morally and eschatologically. And this means that we can never really move on from things, despite the kudos that would seem to reside in saying that we could. Try as we might, there is, for example, no such thing to us as casual sex, discarded afterwards like a smoked cigarette. Now don't get me wrong: I know that there are whole libraries of non-fiction accounts of sex's subject matter to encourage us to think that there is. But the fact is that no amount of unblushing biological knowledge will get you off the hook of it afterwards: for the deeper truth will prove to be that you never went looking for anything so casual in the first place. And why you did not, is because life, love, sex, death – all of these are things we experience fictionally, standing beside ourselves at the same time as we act them out, conducting the literary analysis of 'Why?' and 'Whither?' This is how fiction fights back against non-fiction. We call it self-consciousness. We don't just walk in our moving parts: we walk and at the same time we walk beside ourselves. And here comes a point I have been making throughout this book, but especially in Chapter 3: this distance between us walking in our moving parts and us walking beside ourselves is the space of what I called there 'THE question'.[11] And it should be obvious that sexual activity would be the most potent, or pure, form of this experience; for there is no other experience where the whole pleasure of the thing is the momentary dismissal of our (embarrassing) observing (fictional) selves. Let us be clear about this: the whole pleasure of the thing is not a quantity of pleasure on the scale of such things. Western sexual ethics has been consistently wrong about this. No, the whole pleasure of the thing is not really about pleasure at all, if pleasure can also be eating all the cake or standing on top of the mountain. What we call the whole pleasure of the thing is really the sensation of having our fictional self banished from the room so that we can be left to exist wholly in the blessed irreversibility of the physical event. If you could somehow be made to exist as wholly in the irreversibility of a billiard ball rolling certainly into its pocket, you would experience the same degree of 'pleasure' (or relief) from it. As D. H. Lawrence once put it in a poem:

> There, at the axis
> Pain, or love, or grief
> Sleep on speed; in dead certainty;
> Pure relief.[12]

This explains, finally, why non-fiction cannot prove fiction, why the natural cannot prove the supernatural. In this world, only non-fiction exists, only non-fiction is true. A bullet really will kill you and no amount of wishful thinking can prevent that. Our fictional selves cannot compete with that; and one day there will come a time when they give up trying. The natural is something that we can only prove as we slip towards its unconsciousness (like the Presocratics did).

I believe it is like this. The fact that our fictional selves can ask THE question of 'Why? or 'Whither?' proves that there is another world – and that it is only from the point of view of that other world that this world can be proved to exist.

This is why the child's perspective and make-believe should have the prominence that I have given them within the history of Western philosophy. Because this is a history that has always been written as though it should be taught patiently to children and slaves like a bedtime story. As Heraclitus noted,

> A man is thought as foolish by a supernatural being as a child is by a man.[13]

And yet the children and slaves know what they want: and in that knowing is the answer to everything. It's like Hans Christian Andersen put it:

> There was a young Prince; no one had so many and such beautiful books as he had. He could read in them the history of all the events which have ever happened in the world, and also see them represented in splendid pictures. He could gain from his books all the information he wanted about any country, or people whatsoever.
> But there was not in them a word of what he most desired to know, viz., where the Garden of Paradise was to be found.[14]

The fatal masks

Who wears the *fatal masks*? Answer: Men and Women wear the *fatal masks*.

If they can leave childhood behind for good, adults might find that they have entered upon a game – and this would be a game which should be familiar to all of us. It is the game where sex meets philosophy. It is the game where men *and* women participate in philosophy; that is to say, not just men. And at once we must be aware of a critical fact. This game is coterminous with the Western mind's discovery of objective truth, because it only makes sense with reference to the possibility of that truth. When present-day women philosophers look to shame their male counterparts, it is with reference to the fact that the truth is a sexless entity, the same to any human with the brain to apprehend it. The jealous hoarding of this entity by men for so many years has been the crime which an enlightened Western philosophy would now name and shame and move beyond. We can now say that this game therefore began with the Presocratics.

Before the birth of philosophy, men (but not all) had of course used other means to dominate women. But with the birth of philosophy in the West, this would change forever because here was suddenly the florescence of a highest form of wisdom with which women could demonstrate to be equally adept. Before, if a man chose to abuse a woman with the physical superiority of his body, he was safe within that exercise's own logic. A better man might choose not to do it; but a worse man might do it and prove to everyone's satisfaction that in a brute world, physical superiority has to be its own mandate to rule. The poor woman might object, but then she would be objecting to the fact of a brute world and not the man. I do not need to give historical examples of the weary acquiescence that women steadily acquired over time: for these have been well enough documented by the great feminist writers. What I want to do now is to ask us to imagine the dramatic difference that the birth of philosophy must have made in the West. Here was a precious discovery – more precious than gold and silver – and so man's first instinct must have been to keep it to himself. Let me zoom out briefly to make it over to the next point.

There has always been a point of view to say that the birth of philosophy only happened in ancient Greece when it did because there and there only did you have the necessary material conditions of highly stratified and self-sufficient city-states, benefitting from an enormous slave underclass. There, for the first time, you had a cadre of upper-class males with comparatively little to do of hands-on manual labour. So instead they consorted with each other and drank and talked and thought. The ancient Greek world relied on trade through the Mediterranean and overland from the East: thus to the fuel of friendly banter could be added the pure oxygen of tales of far-off peoples – far-off peoples with their different customs and beliefs and knowledge. This was the splitting of the atom; for it was effectively the discovery that what men have always called 'truth' must go deeper and purer than anyone had previously thought. When you have had no contact with other peoples, you have no reason not to believe that your charmed circle of use and wont is the whole world and that world's truth. Then you encounter another world and its truth; and because of this you are made to realize that what both worlds thought was foundational in their cultures was merely conventional, so that the real truth must be some lowest common denominator of the two or something yet deeper altogether. We can therefore say that it was no chance at all that Thales hailed from Miletus, with its exceptional trading links West and East.[15] So in other words, philosophy in the West began with all the conditions and equipment to make it just another male sport. And yet there was something decidedly different about this sport to make it that the traditional segregation couldn't last long. Men who talk to men also talk to women, their wives and daughters and mistresses. And there was something about philosophy that made this especially likely to happen. This was that it was the first form of wisdom in the history of the world to be able to reflect well on its beholder. Think about it: the wisdoms of the traditional religions couldn't offer this because they did not make a rational appeal to human understanding. They did not ask your mind to corroborate their brilliance. They simply presented you with rituals and beliefs to be learnt rote (or else). But philosophy was obviously very different, for it offered the mind that could understand it the chance to share in its brilliance. Even today, when you attend a complex lecture in philosophy and come away understanding it, is the satisfaction you feel not predominately the satisfaction of having proved your mind to be up to the task? Is this not the difference that you mark between you and your culture and the cultures of more savage peoples who don't attend lectures but sit in temples, enthralled (like children)? This, then, was why the first philosophers couldn't hold it in. This was why they had to blabber and blog about their great minds to others, and to try to lord it over their women. Except, this thing called philosophy that they had discovered was different – was *fatally* different. It was not a strong-arm skill that a weak arm could never hope to have. It was neither strong nor weak. It was neutral like nothing had ever been neutral before. It took everybody's inborn (supernatural) instinct for truth and carried it off beyond merely material considerations. It caught the men and women by surprise with the fact that it worked with something in men and women that both share equally: Reason. And so it came to pass that it would become the chosen place and language for the final struggle between them.

This is the moment at which we encounter the *fatal masks*. Let me recap. The discovery of objective truth, then objective truth's discovery, in turn, of the human brain's sexless rationality, instantly became the liberating doctrine for men and women. The men, it liberated from religion, myth and superstition. The women, it liberated from man's low opinion of them. And nothing has altered this trajectory to the present day. This is still how the questions and problems are formulated. However, if we choose now to deploy the materials of this book, we may find that we reach a new conclusion. That we do is because we have done such extensive work to counter Reason with Freedom – namely, the freedom of the human soul to draw on its supernatural resources and to dream its dreams. Then following that, its freedom to take those same dreams and to hurl them to shatter against the all-sneering imperatives of knowledge. Knowledge and all its lieutenants – the lieutenants named by Wilfred Owen in his poem as 'Fortune, Chance, Necessity, and Death'.[16] This is why I have gone so far in this book to try to describe and re-describe what you call the truth as what I call the will. What I call the *free* will. Because that is as much as a supernatural truth in this natural world can mean. It is something that you have to be continuously expressing as onward-rushing oblivion into the hard materials of life. This, too, is why all human word-assemblies are meaningless; for it turns out that the devilry of silence has all along been waiting to replace them anyway with physics' understanding of itself, so that the meaning of all human language is simply the sheer noise of it while it can last. The collective purpose of human life on earth is to be the means of releasing truth so that it can return to the other world. I think I said like butterflies. Our collective purpose as a species is to flourish for a fractional period of geological time as Nature's conscience. We must be soulful lovers who are all the time being struck by the beauty that exists in this world and in each other's bodies. And we must be aware that for each and every expression of our praise, there will be a corresponding scientific fact that will immediately explain it away. And I think I have made it abundantly clear that the sum total of the scientific facts in the world *is* irresistible and *will* explain our praise away. The only thing for us to do is to take our word of praise and hurl it against the corresponding fact and rest secure in the knowledge that the truth that we felt in our emotion of praise can take care of itself once we have released it through this shattering; because it has another world to escape to.

If all of this is so, then the historical reason for the *fatal masks* becomes clear. On the one hand, we have the liberating discovery that the philosopher's truth is, essentially, sexless. But on the other hand, we have the unaffected fact of the sexes of male and female. To quote again Parmenides from Chapter 1:

> On the right boys, on the left girls...[17]

You hardly need me to tell you how things have developed since then among liberated men and women. The goal has been to reconcile these incompatible facts of sexless truth and sexed humanity in an authentic difference of experience based upon equal-access rights to a single rationality. Feminism has leveraged itself against its belief that theoretical thinking has been man's (unthinking) privilege of default, so that woman's conquest of the same domain should consequently be able to brandish some unmistakable property that sets it off from the male. But how to do this when the domain is – after all – the same? How can two people possess the same truth sufficiently differently? Does a boy dress it up like a boy, and a girl dress it up like a girl? Are these the *fatal masks*? I think they may be. In fact, I think you can see it already in the philosophy of Phintys of Sparta, about whom we know little, other than that she was a Pythagorean and probably an older contemporary of Plato's. She writes remarkably frankly about what it was like back then to be a woman and a philosopher – but watch most of all for the *mask*, and how she lifts it up to cover her face:

> A woman must be altogether good and orderly; without excellence she would never become so. The excellence appropriate to each thing makes superior that which is receptive of it: the excellence appropriate to the eyes makes the eyes so, that appropriate to hearing, the faculty of hearing, that appropriate to a horse, a horse, that appropriate to a man, a man. So too the excellence appropriate to a woman makes a woman excellent. The excellence most appropriate to a woman is moderation. For, on account of this virtue, she will be able to honor and love her husband.
>
> Now many, perhaps, may think it is not fitting for a woman to philosophize, just as it is not fitting for her to ride horses

or speak in public. But I think that some things are peculiar to a man, some to a woman, some are common to both, some belong more to a man than a woman, some more to a woman than a man. Peculiar to a man are serving in battle, political activity, and public speaking; peculiar to a woman are staying at home and indoors, and welcoming and serving her husband. But I say that courage and justice and wisdom are common to both. Excellences of the body are appropriate for both a man and a woman, likewise those of the soul. And just as it is beneficial for the body of each to be healthy, so too, it is beneficial for the soul to be healthy. The excellences of the body are health, strength, keenness of perception and beauty. Some of these are more fitting for a man to cultivate and possess, some more for a woman. For courage and wisdom are more appropriate for a man, both because of his constitution of body and because of his strength of soul, while moderation is more appropriate for a woman... I say this comes from five things: First, from piety and reverence concerning her marriage bed; second, from decency with respect to her body; third, from the processions of those from her own household; fourth, from not indulging in mystery rites and celebrations of the festival of Cybele; fifth, from being devout and correct in her sacrifices to the divine.[18]

If men and women could sex their brains and think from out of different rationalities, then I say that these unflattering masks would not arise and hide and replace their personalities. I should so much like to know what Phintys *really* thought about life; as that would be so much better than watching her break her brains here as she tries to account for herself by that tried and trusted sleight of hand – that trick by which philosophers talk about the 'excellence appropriate to each thing', as if that somehow solves the problem of distributing a single truth fairly around multiple different subjects. This is the same tyranny as the tyranny of 'natural law' which would take on its most imperious form in the Christian era. I should so much like to discover the womanhood in Phintys in a line-by-line unfolding kind of way: in the way that each woman has the capacity to teach us womanhood afresh, clean over from the start; and in just the same way that I imagine that each man can do the same for manhood. I would wish for womanhood and manhood to live and die with each discrete life and never to survive being transported over to objectivity and law. I would wish for womanhood and manhood to have to be rediscovered and relearned in each new moment, or something like that; precisely because that is also their only protection from the designs of objectivity and law. The designs of the *fatal masks*.

I want to jump forward now to something from the electric Anaïs Nin and one of her diaries. She is recounting a conversation with Dr. Otto Rank, the Austrian psychoanalyst. By the time of this conversation we are in New York in 1935, in the full beam of psychoanalysis' full disclosure, but I want you to watch how nothing has really changed. The language and its scenery have been transported to a new height of delicacy, but what I am calling the real problem continues unnoticed and untreated; because what I am calling the real problem is the same thing as the structure of the conversation itself. The conversation is full of good and earnest intent, but that worthy energy has only allowed it to drive deeper into the place where Phintys fell. This is the place where woman racks her brains and tries to explain herself and excuse herself and make up for an eternity of lost time. Nin wants so very much to be able to dismiss man's traditional magnanimity towards woman's traditional intuition. But she is trapped by the fact that what she wants to say must pass through a single corridor that has remained the same since Phintys' day. This corridor prescribes that, when it comes, her dismissal's victory will show that men and women have all along been exactly equal in respect of their abject slavery to a single truth. I'll be frank: it hurts me and angers me to see a great writer like Nin toy with things like that. But read it for yourself:

> Before Rank left for the West, our last conversation was about my assertion that woman's notorious inadequacy in grasping ideas was only relative. She could not grasp abstract ideas, but she was able to transpose them by humanizing or rather personifying them. But once they were embodied, concretized in a person, then she grasped them perhaps more profoundly, because she grasped and experienced them emotionally, and they could affect and transform her. But they are the same ideas which move men through their minds.
>
> Now analysis is revealing how little objectivity there is in man's thinking. Even in the most rational man, there is a fund

of irrational motivations which are personal, and belong to his personal past, to his emotional traumas. So in the end, pure thought rarely exists in its abstract form, it is part of the experience and of the emotions. A synthesis. Invention, discovery, creation, history and philosophy are composed of all these elements. Man generalizes from experience, and denies the source of his generalizations. Woman individualizes and personalizes, but ultimately analysis will reveal that the rationalizations of man are a disguise to his personal bias, and that woman's intuition was nothing more than a recognition of the influence of the personal in all thought.[19]

Let me tell you how it all comes out. First the natural world invents the other world, which is the supernatural world, or the Garden of Paradise – and it invents it in order to put it to death. Second, civilization invents the savage – and it invents him in order to put him to death. Third, philosophy invents religion – and it invents it in order to put it to death. Then fourth, the West invents Socrates – and it invents him in order to put him to death. Finally, *Truth* invents man and woman in its own image. The arrow of this whole process runs ancient to modern – and I have argued that the modern always invents the ancient. The trauma and consequence of knowledge is that it proves beyond a shadow of doubt that all of this is exactly so. Don't believe all that fire and brimstone talk about hell. No. They just keep books in hell. Hell keeps the universe's best library. There are no people in hell being boiled alive. It is far worse than that. There are just biographies of people all lined up neatly on shelves, catalogued to perfection. And they are the most brilliant biographies in the world. The biographies that we still write down here merely flap around in conjectures, but these hellish editions are the real stuff. In them each human life becomes what it always was: catatonically, pathetically, obvious. Dead paper between dead covers. You think that what Nin and the psychoanalysts write is obvious? Well then you should read these biographies! Then you would see what obvious looks like. It looks like you shouldn't even have bothered to live in the first place. Read too long among those pages and you might forget what it feels like to take a chance, to fall in love, to start something that is the opposite of invented in advance. You might find yourself voicing Atomism's sure ethic, just like Democritus did:

> He who feels any desire to beget a child seems to me better advised to take it from one of his friends; he will then have a child such as he wishes, for he can choose the kind he wants... But if a man begets his own child, many are the dangers there; for he must make the best of him whatever his nature.[20]

No one has ever contested that the history of Western philosophy is the history of critical thought. To this I hope to have added the warning that critical thought is not innocent, like floating an opinion. It looks back and invents the past and calls that progress. And it looks back and invents the past in exact proportion to how we should be living it in the present. It is in exact competition with *you*. It wants you to die and the biography of you to live forever. So think LIFEBLOOD, then fight back.

NOTES

Chapter 1

1. Henry Kissinger, *The White House Years* (New York: London, Weidenfeld & Nicolson and Michael Joseph, 1979), p. 229.
2. Aristotle, *Metaphysics*, 983*b* (trans. Richard Hope).
3. See the pioneering work of recovery done by Professor Mary Ellen Waithe in her book (as Editor) *A History of Women Philosophers*, Volume 1, 600 B.C.–500 A.D. (Dordrecht: Martinus Nijhoff Publishers, 1987).
4. Found in Simplicius, *Physics*, XXXIX, 14 & XXXI, 13 (trans. J. E. Raven).
5. Found in Galen, *Hipp. Epid.*, VI, 48 (trans. J. E. Raven).
6. For more on this, see G. M. Mullett, *Spider Woman Stories: Legends of the Hopi Indians* (Tucson, AR: University of Arizona Press, 1979).
7. Ernest Hemingway, 'A Natural History of the Dead', in *The First Forty-Nine Stories* (London: Arrow, 1993), pp. 418–419.
8. A. Martin and O. Primavesi, *L'empédocle de Strasbourg* (P. Strasb. Gr. Inv. 1665–6). Introduction, Édition, Commentaire (Berlin and New York: Walter de Gruyter, 1998), a(ii)18–30.
9. Found in Heraclitus Homericus, *Quaestiones Homericae*, XXII (trans. G. S. Kirk).
10. Found in Aristotle, *De anima*, 405*a* (trans. G. S. Kirk).
11. Found in Aetius, *Opinions*, I, 7, 11 (trans. G. S. Kirk).
12. A. C. Grayling, *The God Argument: The Case against Religion and for Humanism* (London and New York: Bloomsbury, 2013), p. 2.
13. Elspeth Huxley, *The Flame Trees of Thika* (London: Penguin, 1988), p. 128.
14. Frantz Fanon (trans. Constance Farrington), *The Wretched of the Earth* (Harmondsworth: Penguin, 1969), p. 253.
15. R. H. Tawney, *Religion and the Rise of Capitalism* (London: John Murray, 1926), p. 283.
16. Hannah Arendt, *Between Past and Future* (New York: The Viking Press, 1968), p. 157.

17   See Charles Gore, *The Philosophy of the Good Life: Being the Gifford Lectures Delivered in the University of St. Andrews, 1929–30* (London: John Murray, 1930), pp. 339–340:

> [T]he great attempt to form a 'Weltanschaung,' or general conception of the universe, can never be abandoned; but it will never be attained by the arrogance of specialists in any one abstract science or group of sciences seeking to dominate the whole field. And even the more modest minds, which are content to take the findings of different departments from those who in these departments command the most respect, will be always found acknowledging that the vision of the whole in any adequate sense is something very far above their attainments. 'Relativity' and 'abstractness' remain the dominant characteristics of human knowledge, properly so called. The ideal of 'reasonableness' is then a reasonable faith, which welcomes all the light it can get from any quarter, which is enthusiastic for the liberty of enquiring in all directions, which could not tolerate the rejection of anything that can make a valid claim to be called knowledge, on account of moral or religious scruples or prejudices, but yet recognizes faith as the very foundation of reason and the central light of the soul. And this reasonable faith finds its fullest satisfaction in the acceptance of Jesus Christ as the very word of God incarnate.

18   The main Continental influence on Cornford's work in this book came through Emile Durkheim and the sociology journal founded by him and his colleagues, *L'Année Sociologique*. Particular studies of Durkheim's that Cornford mentions include 'Représentations individuelles et representations collectives', *Revue de Metaph. et de Morale*, vi (1898); 'Sociologie religieuse et théorie de la connaissance', *Revue de Metaph. et de Morale*, xvii (1909); and his *De la division du travail social*, Ed. 3 (Paris, F. Alcan, 1911). He also mentions Lucien Lévy-Bruhl, and his *Les fonctions mentales dans les sociétés inférieures* (Paris: Les Presses Universitaires de France, 1910).

19   Perhaps no one today has done more prominent work in this direction than Richard Dawkins – so here is something to consider, then, from his *The God Delusion*:

> Human thoughts and emotions *emerge* from exceedingly complex interconnections of physical entities within the brain. An atheist in this sense of philosophical naturalist is somebody who believes there is nothing beyond the natural, physical world, no *supernatural* creative intelligence lurking behind the observable

universe, no soul that outlasts the body and no miracles – except in the sense of natural phenomena that we don't yet understand. If there is something that appears to lie beyond the natural world as it is now imperfectly understood, we hope eventually to understand it and embrace it within the natural. As ever when we unweave a rainbow, it will not become less wonderful. (Richard Dawkins, *The God Delusion* (London: Transworld, 2007), pp. 34–35)

20 Tertullian, *De carne Christi*, V, 4.
21 Francis Macdonald Cornford, *From Religion to Philosophy: A Study in the Origins of Western Speculation* (New York: Dover Publications, 2004), vii–x.
22 Homer (trans. E. V. Rieu), *The Odyssey* (Harmondsworth: Penguin, 1963), Book XVII, pp. 271–272.
23 Gilbert Murray, *Five Stages of Greek Religion* (Oxford: The Clarendon Press, 1925), pp. 95–96.
24 As Indro Montanelli rather phlegmatically observed in his *Storia dei Greci*, 'Homer said that the Achaeans [Mycenaeans] were a race of outstanding physical beauty. According to him, their men were all athletes, and their women were all beauty queens. This is probably not quite true' (Indro Montanelli, *Storia dei Greci* (Milan: Rizzoli Editore, 1967), p. 37). Author's translation.
25 Hesiod, *Theogony*, II, 211–225 (trans. Hugh G. Evelyn-White).
26 Thucydides, *History of the Peloponnesian War*, II, 38–39 (trans. A. N. W. Saunders).
27 Ibid., II, 41.
28 There is still no better statement that ties all these elements together than Cicero's, from his *De Republica*, III, 22, 33:

> True law is right reason in agreement with Nature; it is of universal application, unchanging and everlasting; it summons to duty by its commands, and averts from wrongdoing by its prohibitions. And it does not lay its commands or prohibitions upon good men in vain, though neither have any effect on the wicked. It is a sin to try to alter this law, nor is it allowable to attempt to repeal any part of it, and it is impossible to abolish it entirely. We cannot be freed from its obligations by Senate or People, and we need not look outside ourselves for an expounder or interpreter of it. And there will not be different laws at Rome and Athens, or different laws now and in the future, but one eternal and unchangeable law will be valid for all nations and for all times, and there will be one master and one ruler, that is, God, over us all, for He is the author of this law, its promulgator, and its enforcing judge.

29 Wernher von Braun, 'Transcription of Dr. Wernher von Braun following Apollo XI mission at Madison County Courthouse, 1969', *Marshall Space Flight Center History Office* [http://history.msfc.nasa.gov/vonbraun/documents/remarks_following_apollo_11.pdf]. Accessed 16 January 2014.
30 Walt Whitman, 'I Sing the Body Electric'.
31 Blaise Pascal, *Pensées*, II, 271.
32 See, for example, the following from his *Leviathan*, XLVI:

> For it is upon this ground [of separated essences], that when a man is dead and buried, they say his soul (that is his life) can walk separated from his body, and is seen by night upon the graves. Upon the same ground they say, that the figure, and colour, and taste of a piece of bread, has a being, there, where they say there is no bread: and upon the same ground they say, that faith, and wisdom, and other virtues are sometimes *poured* into a man, sometimes *blown* into him from Heaven; as if the virtuous, and their virtues could be asunder; and a great many other things that serve to lessen the dependence of subjects on the sovereign power of their country. For who will endeavour to obey the laws, if he expect obedience to be poured or blown into him? Or who will not obey a priest, that can make God, rather than his sovereign; nay than God Himself? Or who, that is in fear of ghosts, will not bear great respect to those that can make the holy water, that drives them from him? And this shall suffice for an example of the errors, which are brought into the church, from the *entities*, and *essences* of Aristotle; which it may be he knew to be false philosophy; but writ it as a thing consonant to, and corroborative of their religion; and fearing the fate of Socrates ... (trans. Stuart Hampshire)

33 Virginia Woolf, *Three Guineas* (New York: Harcourt, 2006), p. 126.

Chapter 2

1 John of Salisbury, *Policraticus*, III, 14 (trans. Joseph B. Pike).
2 Diodorus Siculus, *Bibliotecha historica*, XVI, 27 (trans. Charles L. Sherman).
3 Plato, *Republic*, 511*b–c* (trans. Richard W. Sterling & William C. Scott).
4 Plato, *Republic*, 476*c–d* (trans. F. M. Cornford).

5   See, for instance, how Plato puts it at *Epistles*, VII, 341c:

> There does not exist, and there never shall, any treatise by myself on these matters. The subject does not admit, as the sciences in general do, of exposition. It is only after long association in the great business itself and a shared life that a light breaks out in the soul, kindled, so to say, by a leaping flame, and thereafter feeds itself. (trans. A. E. Taylor)

6   Francis Bacon, *The Works of Francis Bacon*, 12 (London: M. Jones, 1815), p. 48.
7   Augustine, *Confessions*, X, 8, 15 (author's translation).
8   Augustine, *En. in Ps.*, XCVIII, 3 (author's translation).
9   Plato, *Republic*, 516d (trans. Richard W. Sterling & William C. Scott).
10 Ibid., 517b–c; 519e–d (trans. Richard W. Sterling & William C. Scott).
11 Ludwig Wittgenstein, 'A Lecture on Ethics', *The Philosophical Review* 74, no. 1 (1965): 7.
12 Charles Darwin, *On the Origin of Species* (London: Cassell & Co., 1909), p. 64.
13 Mikhail Bulgakov (trans. Carl R. Proffer), 'Diaboliad', in *Diaboliad and Other Stories* (New York: Ardis Publishers, 2012), p. 17.
14 As I have contrasted the creative violence of Art against Natural Selection's claim to have been there all along, I will offer an example of Habermas' project as it directs itself to the problem of Art. Aesthetic appreciation, or aesthetic criticism, has the potential to be an awkward test case for Western rationality. In relation, say, to science, Art can be anything up to a completely random bursting forth of inner, creative energy. But that would make it unclassifiable, when the secret dream of Western rationality is that everything really is classifiable – that is we become types of ourselves, standing self-consciously next to ourselves, and that this deadness is meant to be superior to the living *us*. Instead of the clash of aesthetics, or the clash of civilizations, or whatever you want to call it, there is this weird anaesthetized deadness of spirit. As though the very fight in you were being described back to you, and all its originality turned into 'reasons', all so that you can be retaliated on with the information that all you did was exhibit a legitimate instance of aesthetic appreciation/criticism. Yes: this is a tactic to ignore, in the end, the content of your voice. Yes: if you were motivated to speak towards something because of love, this will seem like a monstrous betrayal. And finally, yes: it is altogether just like adults

treat children. From Habermas' *The Theory of Communicative Action*: 'In practical discourse reasons or grounds are meant to show that a norm recommended for acceptance expresses a generalizable interest; in aesthetic criticism grounds or reasons serve to guide perception and to make the authenticity of a work so evident that this aesthetic experience can itself become a rational motive for accepting the corresponding standards of value' (Jürgen Habermas (trans. Thomas McCarthy), *The Theory of Communicative Action*, Vol. I, *Reason and the Rationalization of Society* (Boston: Beacon Press, 1984), p. 20). What a lifetime away this is from R. G. Collingwood's insight that 'The artistic activity does not use a ready-made language, it "creates" language as it goes along' (R. G. Collingwood, *The Principles of Art* (New York: Oxford University Press, 1968), p. 275).
15 Found in Hippolytus, *Refutation of All Heresies*, IX, 9, 4 (trans. John Burnet).
16 An excellent recent example of this would be Robert Nozick's 'evolutionary' perspective on rationality:

> Rationality is an evolutionary adaption with a delimited purpose and function. It was selected for and designed to work in tandem with enduring facts that held during the period of human evolution, whether or not people could rationally demonstrate these facts. Many of philosophy's traditional intractable problems, resistant to rational resolution, may result from attempts to extend rationality beyond this delimited function. (Robert Nozick, *The Nature of Rationality* (Princeton, NJ: Princeton University Press, 1995), p. 176)

Cf. How L. S. Stebbing puts the same idea:

> There seems to be a deep-rooted tendency in the human mind to seek... something that persists through change. Consequently the desire for explanation seems to be satisfied only by the discovery that what appears to be new and different was there all the time. Hence the search for an underlying identity, a persistent stuff, a substance that is conserved in spite of qualitative changes and in terms of which these changes can be explained. (L. S. Stebbing, *A Modern Introduction to Logic* (London: Methuen, 1930), p. 404)

17 Aristotle, *Metaphysics*, 983*b* (trans. Richard Hope).
18 Ibid., 983*b*–984*a*.

19 Found in Seneca, *Naturales Quaestiones*, III, 14 (trans. G. S. Kirk).
20 Herodotus, *Histories*, II, 178.
21 Ibid., I, 170.
22 Ibid., I, 75.
23 See Acts 17.16-34.
24 See A. E. Taylor, *Elements of Metaphysics* (London: Methuen & Co., 1930), pp. 236–240.
25 George Plekhanov, *The Role of the Individual in History* (New York: International Publishers, 1940), pp. 18–19.
26 This is not also an argument for the 'alternative pre-histories' of civilization that want to say that some of the standout achievements of human ingenuity (say the Sphinx or Machu Picchu) are far older than we actually think they are. So that it turns out that the really distant ancients weren't as simple as we had thought. And by the way there is a growing literature in this line. I am not looking for material proof like this; and nor do I think that my case could be settled by it. Material achievements such as these are proof that states of technical knowledge do, and should, accumulate over time. I, on the other hand, am attacking the belief that such visible achievements of the human hand signify quantitative, pathological improvements to the human animal.
27 Found in Sextus, *Against the Mathematicians*, IX, 193 (trans. John Burnet).
28 Found in Clement, *Stromata*, V, 109, 2 (trans. John Burnet).
29 Ibid., VII, 22, 1 (trans. John Burnet).
30 Ibid., V, 109, 3 (trans. John Burnet).
31 Ibid., V, 109, 1 (trans. John Burnet).
32 Found in Simplicius, *Physics*, XXIII, 11 & XXIII, 20 (trans. G. S. Kirk).
33 Ibid., XXXV, 3 (trans. G. S. Kirk).
34 I am referring, of course, to his classification and removal of the 'ecclesiastical principality' from his historical survey of human socio-political behaviour:

> It now remains to discuss ecclesiastical principalities; and here the difficulties which have to be faced occur before the ruler is established, in that such principalities are won by prowess or by fortune, but are kept without the help of either. They are maintained, in fact, by religious institutions, of such a powerful kind that, no matter how the ruler acts and lives, they safeguard his government. Ecclesiastical princes alone possess states, and do not defend them; subjects and do not govern them. And as their

states are not defended they are not taken away from them; and their subjects, being without government, do not worry about it and neither can nor hope to overthrow it in favour of another. So these principalities alone are secure and happy. But as they are sustained by higher powers which the human mind cannot comprehend, I shall not argue about them; they are exalted and maintained by God, and so only a rash and presumptuous man would take it upon himself to discuss them. (Niccolò Machiavelli (trans. George Bull) *The Prince* (Harmondsworth: Penguin, 1970), pp. 73–74)

35 Bertrand Russell (ed. Paul Edwards), *Why I Am Not a Christian* (New York: Simon & Schuster, 1957), pp. 111–115.

Chapter 3

1 Giambattista Vico (trans. Thomas Goddard Bergin & Max Harold Fisch), *The New Science of Giambattista Vico* (Ithaca and London: Cornell University Press, 1984).
2 Charles Baudelaire, 'Correspondances' (trans. Lewis Piaget Shanks).
3 See Vico, *The New Science*, §31, p. 20:

> ... (1) The age of the gods, in which the gentiles believed they lived under divine governments, and everything was commanded them by auspices and oracles, which are the oldest institutions in profane history. (2) The age of the heroes, in which they reigned everywhere in aristocratic commonwealths, on account of a certain superiority of nature which they held themselves to have over the plebs. (3) The age of men, in which all men recognized themselves as equal in human nature, and therefore there were established first the popular commonwealths and then the monarchies, both of which are forms of human government.

4 Ibid., §1096, pp. 414–415.
5 Rene Descartes (trans. R. P. Miller), *Principles of Philosophy* (Boston: Kluwer Academic Publishers, 1984), xxiv.
6 Vico, *The New Science*, §357, p. 106.
7 See Ibid., §394, p. 124:

> The three princes of this doctrine, Hugo Grotius, John Selden, and Samuel von Pufendorf, should have taken their start from the

beginnings of the gentes, where their subject matter begins. But all three of them err together in this respect, by beginning in the middle; that is, with the latest times of the civilized nations (and thus more enlightened by fully developed reason), from which the philosophers emerged and rose to meditation of a perfect idea of justice.

8   Ibid., §186–187, p. 71.
9   Ibid., §1406, pp. 427–428.
10 Ibid., §405, pp. 129–130.
11 H. A. L. Fisher, *A History of Europe* (London: Edward Arnold & Co., 1949), v.
12 Vico, *The New Science*, §1108, p. 425.
13 Ibid., §349, pp. 104–105.
14 Plato (trans. Benjamin Jowett), *Euthyphro* (Oxford: The Clarendon Press, 1903), 17–18.
15 Aristotle, *Politics*, 1253*a* (trans. Ernest Barker).
16 See how I make this point in relation to Hobbes in Chapter 1, pp. 37–38.
17 Plato, *Apology*, 19*a* (trans. Benjamin Jowett).
18 Plato, *Phaedrus*, 230*e* (trans. Benjamin Jowett).
19 Ibid., 276*b–c*.
20 T. E. Lawrence, *Seven Pillars of Wisdom* (London: Penguin, 2000), pp. 288–289.
21 Eccles. 9.1–2.
22 Something that is evident from Boole's own identification of what he calls 'a certain just supremacy of truth' – see George Boole, *An Investigation of the Laws of Thought* (New York: Cosimo, 2007), p. 408:

> Where, then, the laws of valid reasoning are uniformly obeyed, a very close parallelism would exist between the operations of the intellect and those of Nature. Subjection to laws mathematical in their form and expression, even the subjection of an absolute obedience, would stamp upon the two series one common character. The reign of necessity over the intellectual and the physical world would be alike complete and universal. But while the observation of external Nature testifies with ever-strengthening evidence to the fact, that uniformity of operation and unvarying obedience to appointed laws prevail throughout her entire domain, the slightest attention to the processes of the intellectual world reveals to us another state of things. The mathematical laws of reasoning are, properly speaking, the laws of *right* reasoning only, and their actual transgression is a

perpetually recurring phenomenon. Error, which has no place in the material system, occupies a large one here. We must accept this as one of those ultimate facts, the origin of which it lies beyond the province of our science to determine... If we regard the intellect as free, and this is apparently the view most in accordance with the general spirit of these speculations, its freedom must be viewed as opposed to the dominion of necessity, not to the existence of a certain just supremacy of truth. The laws of correct inference may be violated, but they do not the less truly *exist* on this account.

23 See Chapter 1, p. 35.
24 Vico, *The New Science*, §1095, p. 414.
25 Ibid., §383–384, p. 120.
26 Mao Tse-tung, *On Practice: On the Relation Between Knowledge and Practice – Knowing and Doing* (Peking: Foreign Languages Press, 1964), pp. 8–9.
27 Vico, *The New Science*, §375, pp. 116–117.
28 Georges Bataille (trans. Kathleen Raine), *L'expérience intérieure* (Paris: Gallimard, 1943), p. 109.
29 Johann Wolfgang von Goethe, *Faust Part One* (trans. John Anster).
30 Louis Guilloux, *La maison du people* (Paris: Grasset & Fasquelle, 2004), p. 16 (author's translation).
31 Steven Pinker, 'Science Is Not Your Enemy: An Impassioned Plea to Neglected Novelists, Embattled Professors, and Tenure-less Historians', *New Republic*, 6 August 2013, paras 15 & 33.
32 See Chapter 1, pp. 12–13.
33 Found in Aristotle, *De anima*, 405*a* (trans. G. S. Kirk).
34 Found in Diogenes Laertius, I, 24 (trans. G. S. Kirk). Note: Amber is mentioned as it was known to the ancients to be able to attract feathers after having been rubbed with fur. This was of course due to its capacity to take an electrostatic charge – something first explained in the seventeenth century by the astronomer William Gilbert.
35 Found in Aristotle, *De anima*, 411*a* (trans. G. S. Kirk).
36 Found in Plato, *Laws*, X, 899*b* (trans. A. E. Taylor).
37 Found in Aetius, *Opinions*, I, 7, 11 (trans. G. S. Kirk).
38 See Chapter 2, pp. 63–65.
39 Found in Diogenes Laertius, *Lives of Famous Philosophers*, II, 1–2 (trans. G. S. Kirk).
40 Christopher Marlowe, *Tragical History of Dr. Faustus* (Oxford: Oxford University Press, 1907), pp. 68–69.
41 Found in Simplicius, *Physica Ascultatio*, XXIV, 13 (trans. G. S. Kirk).

42 Seneca, *De Ira*, II, 27, 2 (author's translation).
43 Anon, from 'Seventeen Old Poems', n. 6, in Arthur Waley, *Chinese Poems* (London: George Allen & Unwin, 1946), p. 59.
44 Found in Apollonius, *Enquiry into Miracles*, 6.2e (trans. Robin Waterfield).
45 See Chapter 1, p. 21.
46 See A. C. Bouquet, *Comparative Religion* (London: Cassell, 1961), p. 12:

> Thus we have the *hodos*, or way, of the Pharisees. Early Christianity in the Book of Acts is called "that Way"; Buddhism is described as "the noble eight-fold path"; and Japanese nationalist *religion* (if we must use the European label) is called Shinto, "the Way of the God": while Communist Russia, true to her semi-Oriental ancestry, has for the time being rejected Theism (or rather the European term "religion") in favour of surrender to the Dialectical Process – which is again a "Way". Confucius' message is called by him "The Way".

47 Found in Sextus, *Against the Mathematicians*, VII, 49 & 110 (trans. John Burnet).
48 Found in Plutarch, *Symposiacs*, IX, 7 (trans. John Burnet).
49 Found in Stobaeus, *Anthologium*, I, 8, 2 (trans. G. S. Kirk).
50 Found in Herodian, *On Peculiar Style*, XLI, 5 (trans. John Burnet).
51 Found in Hippolytus, *Refutation of All Heresies*, IX, 10, 6 (trans. G. S. Kirk).
52 Found in Aristotle, *Problemata*, 916a (trans. E. S. Forster).
53 Found in Sextus, *Against the Mathematicians*, VII, 132 (trans. G. S. Kirk).
54 Found in Plutarch, *On Exile*, 604a (trans. Robin Waterfield).
55 Found in Stobaeus, *Anthology*, III, 1, 179 (trans. Robin Waterfield).
56 As Aristotle explained it at *Metaphysics*, 986a,

> [T]he so-called Pythagoreans, the first to be absorbed in mathematics, not only advanced this particular science, but, having been brought up on it, they believed that its principles are the principles of all things. Now, of these principles, numbers are naturally the first. As a result, they seemed to see in numbers, rather than in fire, earth, and water, many similarities to things as they are and as they come to be... In view of all this, they took the elements of numbers to be the elements of all things, and the whole heaven to be in harmony with number. They were adept at finding numbers and harmonies, both in patterns of change and in the structure of parts. (trans. Richard Hope)

57 Found in Proclus, *On Euclid's Elements* [G. Friedlein ed., 1967, p. 65] (trans. J. E. Raven).
58 Found in Diogenes, *Lives of Famous Philosophers*, VIII, 8 (trans. J. E. Raven).
59 Found in Apollonius, *Historiae Mirabiles*, VI (trans. J. E. Raven).
60 Found in Stobaeus, *Anthology*, I, 49, 53 (trans. John Burnet).

Chapter 4

1 Bertrand Russell, *A History of Western Philosophy* (London: George Allen & Unwin, 1946), p. 385.
2 Found in Aristotle, *De anima*, 405a (trans. J. A. Smith).
3 Found in Sextus, *Against the Mathematicians*, VII, 135 (trans. G. S. Kirk).
4 Found in Theophrastus, *De sensu*, LXVI (trans. G. S. Kirk).
5 Found in Galen, *De medicina*, MCCLIX, 8 (trans. G. S. Kirk).
6 Charles Darwin, *On the Origin of Species* (London: Cassell & Co., 1909), p. 410.
7 See William James, *The Principles of Psychology*, vol. 1 (New York, Cosimo, 2007), p. 609:

> In short, the practically cognized present is no knife-edge, but a saddle-back, with a certain breadth of its own on which we sit perched, and from which we look in two directions into time. The unit of composition of our perception of time is a *duration*, with a bow and a stern, as it were – a rearward and a forward-looking end.

8 See Chapter 3, p. 86.
9 Found in Simplicius, *De caelo*, DLVII, 21 (trans. J. E. Raven).
10 See Friedrich Nietzsche (trans. R. J. Hollingdale), *Twilight of the Idols/The Anti-Christ* (London: Penguin Books, 1990), p. 117.
11 See Chapter 3, p. 108.
12 D. H. Lawrence, 'Going back'.
13 Found in Origen, *Against Celsus*, VI, 12, 14–15 (trans. Robin Waterfield).
14 Hans Christian Andersen, 'The Garden of Paradise'.
15 See Chapter 2, pp. 72–73.
16 See Wilfred Owen, 'The Fates': 'They watch me, those informers to the Fates,/Called Fortune, Chance, Necessity, and Death;/Time, in disguise as one who serves and waits,/Eternity, as girls of fragrant breath.'

17 See Chapter 1, p. 10.
18 Phintys of Sparta, quoted in Mary Ellen Waithe (Ed.) *A History of Women Philosophers*, Volume 1, 600 B.C.–500 A.D., pp. 26–27.
19 Anaïs Nin, *The Diary of Anaïs Nin, Volume Two, 1934–39* (New York and London: The Swallow Press, 1967), p. 19.
20 Found in Stobaeus, *Anthologium*, IV, 24, 32 (trans. G. S. Kirk).

BIBLIOGRAPHY

Primary Sources

Burnet, John. *Early Greek Philosophy*. London: A & C Black, 1908.
Freeman, Kathleen. *Ancilla to the Pre-Socratic Philosophers*. Cambridge, MA: Harvard University Press, 1983.
Kirk, G. S. and Raven, J. E. *The Presocratic Philosophers*. Cambridge: Cambridge University Press, 1962.
Waithe, Mary Ellen (ed.), *A History of Women Philosophers, Volume 1, 600 B.C.–500 A.D.* Dordrecht: Martinus Nijhoff Publishers, 1987.
Waterfield, Robin. *The First Philosophers*. Oxford: Oxford University Press, 2009.

Secondary Sources

Barnes, Jonathan. *The Presocratic Philosophers*. London: Routledge, 1983.
Berlin, Isaiah. *Four Essays on Liberty*. Oxford: Oxford University Press, 1969.
Betegh, Gábor. *The Derveni Papyrus: Cosmology, Theology, and Interpretation*. Cambridge: Cambridge University Press, 2004.
Bodenheimer, Edgar. 'The Natural-Law Doctrine Before the Tribunal of Science: A Reply to Hans Kelsen', *The Western Political Quarterly* 3, no. 3 (1951): 335–63.
Bronowski, J. and Mazlish, Bruce. *The Western Intellectual Tradition*. Harmondsworth: Penguin, 1963.
Burkert, Walter. *Lore and Science in Ancient Pythagoreanism*. Translated by E. L. Minar, Jr. Cambridge, MA: Harvard University Press, 1972.
Burnet, John. 'Law and Nature in Greek Ethics', *International Journal of Ethics* 7, no. 3 (1897): 328–33.
Caston, V. and Graham, D. W. (eds.), *Presocratic Philosophy: Essays in Honor of A. P. D. Mourelatos*. Aldershot: Ashgate Publishing Co., 2002.

Cherniss, Harold. *Aristotle's Criticism of Presocratic Philosophy*. Baltimore: John Hopkins University Press, 1952.
Cornford, F. M. *From Religion to Philosophy*. London: Edward Arnold, 1912.
Cornford, F. M. *Before and After Socrates*. Cambridge: Cambridge University Press, 1932.
Cornford, F. M. *Principium Sapentiae*. Cambridge: Cambridge University Press, 1952.
Curd, Patricia. *The Legacy of Parmenides*. Princeton: Princeton University Press, 1998.
Curd, Patricia. 'The Presocratics as Philosophers', In *Qu'est-ce que la philosophie présocratique?* edited by A. Laks and C. Louguet, 115–38. Lille: Presses Universitaires du Septentrion, 2002.
Dancy, R. 'Thales, Anaximander, and Infinity', *Apeiron* 12 (1989): 149–90.
Dodds, E. R. *The Greeks and the Irrational*. Berkeley: University of California Press, 1951.
Finkelberg, A. 'On the History of the Greek Kosmos', *Harvard Studies in Classical Philology* 98 (1998): 103–36.
Frankfort, Henri et al., *Before Philosophy*. Harmondsworth: Penguin, 1961.
Frede, Dorothea and Burkhard Reis. *Body and Soul in Ancient Philosophy*. Berlin: de Gruyter, 2009.
Furley, D. J. *Cosmic Problems: Essays on Greek and Roman Philosophy of Nature*. Cambridge: Cambridge University Press, 1989.
Gadamer, Hans-Georg. *The Beginning of Philosophy*. London and New York: Continuum, 2000.
Gadamer, Hans-Georg. *The Beginning of Knowledge*. London and New York: Continuum, 2003.
Goldin, O. 'Parmenides on Possibility and Thought', *Apeiron* 26 (1993): 19–35.
Graham, D. W. *Explaining the Cosmos: The Ionian Tradition of Scientific Philosophy*. Princeton: Princeton University Press, 2006.
Greene, William Chase. 'Fate, Good, and Evil in Pre-Socratic Philosophy', *Harvard Studies in Classical Philology* 47 (1936): 85–129.
Hermann, A. *To Think Like God. Pythagoras and Parmenides: The Origins of Philosophy*. Las Vegas: Parmenides Publishing, 2004.
Jacobs, David C. (ed.), *Presocratics after Heidegger*. New York: State University of New York Press, 1999.
Jaeger, Werner. *The Theology of the Early Greek Philosophers*. London: Oxford University Press, 1947.
Kahn, Charles H. *Anaximander and the Origins of Greek Cosmology*. New York: Columbia University Press, 1960.
Kahn, Charles H. *Pythagoras and the Pythagoreans*. Indianapolis: Hackett, 2001.
Kahn, Charles H. *Essays on Being*. Oxford: Oxford University Press, 2009.

Kelsen, Hans. 'Natural Law Before the Tribunal of Science', *The Western Political Quarterly* 2, no. 4 (1949): 481–513.
Kenny, Sir Anthony. *A New History of Western Philosophy: Volume 1, Ancient Philosophy.* Oxford: Oxford University Press, 2004.
Kingsley, P. *Ancient Philosophy, Mystery and Magic.* Oxford: Oxford University Press, 1995.
Lesher, J. H. 'Perceiving and Knowing in the Iliad and the Odyssey', *Phronesis* 26 (1981): 2–24.
Lewis, E. 'Anaxagoras and the Seeds of a Physical Theory', *Apeiron* 33 (2000): 1–24.
McDiarmid, John B. 'Theophrastus on the Presocratic Causes', *Harvard Studies in Classical Philology* 61 (1953): 85–156.
McKirahan, R. *Philosophy Before Socrates.* Indianapolis: Hackett Publishing Company, 1994.
Mogyoródi, E. 'Thales and the Beginnings of Greek Philosophical Speculation', *Acta Antiqua Academiae Scientiarum Hungaricae* 40 (2000): 335–48.
Naddaf, G. *The Greek Concept of Nature.* Albany: SUNY, 2005.
Nussbaum, M. 'Psyche in Heraclitus', *Phronesis* 17 (1972): 1–16; 153–70.
Osborne, Catherine. *Rethinking Early Greek Philosophy: Hippolytus of Rome and the Presocratics.* Ithaca, NY: Cornell University Press, 1987.
Owen, G. E. L. *Logic, Science, and Dialectic: Collected Papers in Greek Philosophy.* Ithaca, NY: Cornell University Press, 1986.
Palmer, J. 'Aristotle and the Ancient Theologians', *Apeiron* 33 (2003): 1–10.
Palmer, J. *Parmenides and Presocratic Philosophy.* New York: Oxford University Press, 2010.
Popper, Karl R. *Objective Knowledge: An Evolutionary Approach.* Oxford: The Clarendon Press, 1975.
Popper, Karl R. *The World of Parmenides: Essays on the Presocratic Enlightenment.* London: Routledge, 1998.
Raven, J. E. *Pythagoreans and Eleatics.* Cambridge: Cambridge University Press, 1948.
Snell, Bruno. *The Discovery of the Mind: The Greek Origins of European Thought.* Translated by T. G. Rosenmeyer. New York: Harper & Row, 1960.
Stokes, M. *One and Many in Presocratic Philosophy.* Washington, DC: The Center for Hellenic Studies, 1971.
Taub, L. C. *Ancient Meteorology.* New York: Routledge, 2003.
Tell, H. 'Sages at the Games: Intellectual Displays and Dissemination of Wisdom in Ancient Greece', *Classical Antiquity* 26 (2007): 249–75.
Vernant, Jean-Pierre. *Myth and Thought among the Greeks.* Translated by Janet Lloyd with Jeff Fort. New York: Zone Books, 2006.

Vlastos, Gregory. 'Theology and Philosophy in Early Greek Thought', *Philosophical Quarterly* 2 (1952): 97–123.

Vlastos, Gregory. 'Review of *Principium Sapentiae*, by F. M. Cornford', *Gnomon* 27 (1955): 65–76.

Vlastos, Gregory. *Studies in Greek Philosophy, Vol. I: The Presocratics*, edited by D. Graham, Princeton: Princeton University Press, 1995.

Warren, James. *Presocratics: Natural Philosophers Before Socrates.* Berkeley: University of California Press, 2007.

Wider, Kathleen. 'Women Philosophers in the Ancient Greek World: Donning the Mantle', *Hypatia* 1, no. 1 (1986): 21–62.

Wigans, W. (ed.), *Logos and Muthos: Philosophical Essays in Greek Literature.* Albany: SUNY Press, 2010.

Wright, M. R. *Cosmology in Antiquity.* New York: Routledge, 1995.

INDEX

Adam and Eve 78, 84, 91
Alcmaeon 121–2
Alexander the Great 41
Anaximander 104–14
Andersen, Hans Christian 140
Antinous 23
Arendt, Hannah 16–18, 25
Arignote 8
Aristotle 7, 16, 33, 61–2, 84, 93, 102, 133–4
Augustine, St. 17–18, 48

Bataille, Georges 96
Baudelaire, Charles 73
Blaise, Pascal 30–1
Bouquet, A. C. 117
Braun, Dr Wernher von 28
Bulgakov, Mikhail 58–9
Bushmen, nation of 85

Carroll, Lewis 75
Churchill, Winston Sir 87
Cicero 41
Cornford, F. M. 19–25, 62, 86

Damo 8
Darwin, Charles 19, 31, 56–9, 61, 82, 103, 121, 132
Democritus 128–9, 147–8
Descartes, René 74–6, 99
Diodorus Siculus 42
Diogenes 7–8
Diogenes Laertius 106
Dionides 41

Empedocles 10, 124
Euthyphro 83–4

Fanon, Frantz 15–16, 20
Fisher, H. A. L. 80
Fuegians, the 31

Goethe, Johann Wolfgang von 97
Gore, Charles 19
Grayling, A. C. 12
Grotius, Hugo 76
Guilloux, Louis 98–9, 102, 117–18

Habermas, Jürgen 61
Hemingway, Ernest 10
Heracleitus 60–1, 119, 123, 140
Hesiod 22, 25, 67
Hobbes, Thomas 33, 77
Homer 21–5, 27, 67, 72, 76–7, 93, 118
Hopi, Native American nation of 9
Huxley, Elspeth 14–15, 16

James, William 133
John of Salisbury 41

Keats, John 68–9
Kikuyu, Kenyan tribe 14–15
Kissinger, Henry 6

The Last White Man 42–3, 68, 71
Lawrence, D. H. 139
Lawrence, T. E. 89–90
Leucippus 128

INDEX

Machiavelli, Niccolò 69
Mao Tse-tung 93–4
Marlowe, Christopher 107
Marx, Karl 17, 65, 72, 76
Melissus 131–4
Metaphysic, the Lady 72, 75
Murray, Gilbert 23
Myia 8

Newton, Isaac Sir 31, 113
Nietzsche, Friedrich 136
Nin, Anaïs 146–7
Noah 72

Odysseus 23
Owen, Wilfred 143

Parmenides 8–9, 67–8, 144
Paul, St. 17–18
Pericles 26–8
Perses 22
Philomelus 42
Phintys 144–6
Piltdown Man 87
Pinker, Steven 100–1, 111
Plato 16, 30, 43–68, 82, 83, 85, 86–91, 97, 117, 136, 144
Plekhanov, George 65
Prisoner 56435 119
Pufendorf, Samuel von 76
Pythagoras 8, 113, 123

Rank, Otto Dr 146–7
Russell, Bertrand 68–9, 126

Selden, John 76
Seneca 62, 109, 115
Shakespeare, William 20
Shelley, Percy Bysshe 125
Simplicius 108
Socrates 3–8, 16, 43–63, 68, 82–91, 105, 137, 147
Spider Woman *or* Thinking Woman 9

Tawney, R. H. 16
Taylor, A. E. 65
Tertullian 20
Thales 7–8, 11, 20–1, 22, 61–5, 84, 102–8, 110, 120, 126, 127, 142
Theano 8
Theophrastus 121
Thucydides 26

Vico, Giambattista 31, 71–86, 92–4

Whitman, Walt 1–2, 4, 18, 29, 42
Wittgenstein, Ludwig 37, 55–6, 104
Wordsworth, William 20, 21

Xenophanes 67, 117–18

www.ingramcontent.com/pod-product-compliance
Lightning Source LLC
Chambersburg PA
CBHW061838300426
44115CB00013B/2438